STEPHANIE PEZARD, MICHAEL SHURKIN, DAVID OCHMANEK

A Strong Ally Stretched Thin

An Overview of France's Defense Capabilities from a Burdensharing Perspective

Prepared for the Office of the Secretary of Defense
Approved for public release; distribution unlimited

RAND NATIONAL DEFENSE RESEARCH INSTITUTE

For more information on this publication, visit www.rand.org/t/RRA231-1

Library of Congress Cataloging-in-Publication Data is available for this publication.
ISBN: 978-1-9774-0513-5

Published by the RAND Corporation, Santa Monica, Calif.

Cover: Alamy stock photo

Preface

This research report is part of a larger study on "Understanding and Optimizing Burdensharing: Developing a Deeper Understanding of Allied and Partner Contributions," led by C. King Mallory and David Ochmanek.

The French military is among Western Europe's most capable; in this report, we examine the role that this military might play as a coalition partner in a hypothetical high-intensity conventional conflict in Europe. We drew on a wide range of publications in French and English, as well as on conversations with French defense experts (journalists, think tank staff, and government officials) and uniformed French officers to understand not just the French military's capabilities and capacity to wage war in general but also its ability to wage high-intensity conventional warfare in particular. France's prowess with respect to expeditionary warfare in Africa is well established, but how well can the French fight armored units with peer technology?

Human Subject Protections (HSP) protocols were used in this study in accordance with the appropriate statutes and Department of Defense (DoD) regulations governing HSP. Additionally, the views of the sources rendered anonymous by HSP are solely their own, and do not represent the official policy or position of DoD or the U.S. Government. The research reported here was completed in April 2020 and underwent security review with the sponsor and the Defense Office of Prepublication and Security Review before public release.

This research was sponsored by the Office of the Deputy Assistant Secretary for Strategy and Force Development, Office of the Under Secretary of Defense for Policy, and conducted within the International Security and Defense Policy Center of the RAND National Security Research Division (NSRD), which operates the National Defense

Research Institute (NDRI), a federally funded research and development center sponsored by the Office of the Secretary of Defense, the Joint Staff, the Unified Combatant Commands, the Navy, the Marine Corps, the defense agencies, and the defense intelligence enterprise.

For more information on the RAND International Security and Defense Policy Center Center, see www.rand.org/nsrd/isdp or contact the director (contact information is provided on the webpage).

Contents

Figures and Tables

Figures

Tables

Summary

France currently possesses one of Western Europe's most capable militaries, owing to the country's commitment to maintaining as wide a range of military capabilities as possible and preserving its capacity to handle any kind of conflict, including high-intensity conventional warfare, without the necessity of allies. Like all Western European militaries, the French military has significantly reduced its force structure. Each of France's three services—which are now fully professional, after ending conscription in 1996—are less than half the size they were at the end of the Cold War, when about half of the French military's manpower consisted of conscripts. Inevitably, the reductions in size translated into reductions in capacity. However, the French, because of their strategic priorities, still have a greater range of capabilities than most other European militaries. France's capacity to sustain a high-end, conventional conflict nonetheless is limited. The French military might be able to accomplish all its assigned missions at once, but it lacks depth, meaning that such demanding operations would quickly exhaust both its human and material resources.[1]

French defense strategy is built around several commitments that date to the incumbency of President Charles de Gaulle (1959–1969): maintaining a nuclear arsenal (France possesses the air and submarine legs of the nuclear triad, having given up ground-launched nuclear-tipped missiles in the 1990s); retaining the ability to intervene anytime, anywhere to protect national interests; and protecting key defense

[1] Conversation with senior French defense officials, March 2019; conversation with French researchers on defense issues, March 2019; conversation with senior French defense official C, March 2019.

industries. More recently, France has boosted its defense spending: It has affirmed its commitment to reaching the North Atlantic Treaty Organization (NATO) goal of spending 2 percent of its gross domestic product on defense, making itself a prominent and useful partner in coalition operations.[2]

However, it is important to note that French views on burden-sharing arguably depart from U.S. views; the French consider their military's active overseas operations, especially in the Sahel but also in Iraq and Syria, as burdensharing—a form of in-kind contribution that enhances NATO and European security even when not conducted under a NATO or European Union mandate. Moreover, although the French are concerned about Russian activities on their southern flank (e.g., Libya, Syria), they view the Russian conventional threat in Europe as limited, based on their assessment that nuclear deterrence would likely prevail under such circumstances.[3]

The French Army

The French Army was 300,000 strong at the end of the Cold War, boasting 15 divisions and three separate corps. It had a significant degree of specialization, distinguishing its conventional warfare-geared units from its lighter expeditionary ones. The Army now has only two divisions and is designed to be a multipurpose force, with a focus on what the French refer to as the segment médian (middle segment) of the conflict spectrum. The middle segment is generally defined as heavy enough to survive on a conventional battlefield yet light enough to remain expeditionary—i.e., deployable to austere environments, such as Mali, in the absence of ample logistical capabilities.

The Army has been making major investments in technology, especially networked warfare technology (as seen in the multibillion-

[2] Florence Parly, "The US-French Relationship in a Changing World," speech before the Atlantic Council, Washington D.C., March 18, 2019a.

[3] Conversation with senior French defense official A, March 2019; conversation with senior French defense officials, March 2019.

euro SCORPION modernization program), but it faces a challenge with respect to readiness, owing to past budget cuts and austerity measures, a small number of weapon systems, and the burden of sustaining ongoing overseas operations (most notably Operation Barkhane in the Sahel and the homeland security operation known as Operation Sentinelle). The result is a struggle to conduct training relevant to conventional warfare and to maintain personnel and materiel readiness for any additional contingencies, especially high-intensity conflicts, which would require ample resources and might feature high rates of attrition.

The French Air Force

Like the Army, the French Air Force has retained a broad range of capabilities, although it suffers from limited capacity. One reason for the Air Force's strength is the nation's commitment to nuclear weapons, which obliges France to invest in ensuring it has the means to deliver said weapons. French Rafales are fully interoperable with NATO, and the French are keen on making them interoperable with F-35s.[4] There is a plan to replace the Rafale with a sixth-generation plane by 2035–2040.

However, the French severely lack strategic airlift. The introduction of A330 Multirole Tanker Transports will add strategic airlift ability while relieving overstretched aerial refueling capabilities.[5] Other gaps include a lack of munitions, as well as a lack of suppression of enemy air defenses (SEAD). The latter is also diminished by limited munitions, as SEAD can require firing large numbers of SCALP air-launched or sea-launched cruise missiles. Finally, the Air Force also is struggling with operational readiness. The problem applies to all French military aircraft, but it is particularly pronounced with its rotary-wing fleet (a problem shared with the Army).[6] Fiscal austerity is

---

4 Conversation with senior French defense official D, April 2019.

5 Sénat, Hearing of French Air Force Chief of Staff General Philippe Lavigne on the 2019 Draft Budget Law, October 24, 2018.

6 Michel Cabirol, "Disponibilité des Aéronefs Militaires: C'est Vraiment Très, Très Alarmant!" *La Tribune*, February 20, 2018a.

one cause of this lack of readiness; another is France's frequent deployment of aircraft to demanding environments, especially the Sahel.[7]

The French Navy

The French Navy, like the Air Force, shrank after the Cold War, but it has preserved a number of capabilities, primarily to maintain its nuclear mission.[8] It has shrunk from 75,000 to about 35,000 personnel and from a fleet of 147 combat and support vessels in 1985 to about 90 today. Meanwhile, the Navy has been making major investments to maintain a modern fleet of ballistic missile submarines and protect them.[9] The latter requires a robust antisubmarine capability, which is provided by aircraft, new frigates, and attack submarines.[10] The French have been modernizing their attack and ballistic submarines, as well as the associated weapon systems, while expanding their modern frigate fleet. The Navy recently refitted its lone aircraft carrier, the nuclear-powered *Charles de Gaulle*, and is conducting studies for the construction of one or possibly two carriers to replace it.[11] The Navy also is scheduled to modernize a number of its aircraft, including its carrier-borne E-2 early warning aircraft and its Atlantique patrol craft; the latter do double duty as intelligence, surveillance, and reconnaissance platforms and as weapon platforms supporting land operations in Africa and the Levant.

By and large, French naval personnel are trained for conventional warfare, as the Navy's mission really has not changed since the Cold

---

7 Vincent Lamigeon, "56% des Aéronefs Incapables de Voler : L'Incroyable Talon d'Achille de l'Armée Française," *Challenges*, December 11, 2017.

8 Conversation with French researchers on defense issues, March 2019.

9 See the annex to Patrick Boureille, "L'Outil Naval Français et la Sortie de la Guerre Froide (1985-1994)," *Revue Historique des Armées*, No. 245 December 15, 2006.

10 Conversation with former senior French defense official A, March 2019.

11 The *Charles de Gaulle* is immobilized, on average, every five years for maintenance (Olivier Fourt, "Armée Française: Le Porte-Avions Nucléaire, un Outil Présidentiel," *Radio France International*, November 14, 2018).

War. The Navy's limitations are found in the relatively small size of the fleet. Like France's other services, the Navy has issues with readiness, and munitions stocks reportedly are low.

Space, Cyber, and Intelligence Capabilities

France is making major investments in the space and cyber domains. France regards space as a critical enabler for a host of high-end capabilities, including its nuclear capabilities, and sees cyber capabilities as increasingly necessary for its own defense.[12] France is working on defensive and offensive space capabilities while also modernizing its satellites, often in cooperation with European and other international partners. France's official space strategy calls for continued cooperation with the United States, which it describes as an "essential ally."[13] With regard to cyber capabilities, the French have been responding to an increased threat level—including from Russia—with organizational changes, new doctrines, and new funding. For example, in January 2017, France stood up a cyber operational command tasked with defending military networks and critical infrastructures. The funding also benefits France's intelligence agencies, which all are seeing significant increases in funding and personnel.[14]

Political and Societal Constraints on the Use of Force

France has few legal political constraints against the executive use of force. The French constitution largely places defense policy and control over the military in the control of the directly elected president, and military interventions have historically received strong public support.

---

[12] Conversation with French researchers on defense issues, March 2019.

[13] Ministère des Armées, *Stratégie Spatiale de Défense*, Paris, 2019, p. 38.

[14] Sénat, Hearing of Defense Minister Florence Parly on 2019 Draft Budget Law, October 15, 2018.

France's ability to deploy forces remains constrained, however, by the sheer number of its ongoing operations—overseas (Operation Barkhane), homeland counterterrorism (Operation Sentinelle), nuclear deterrence (for the Navy and Air Force), and the maritime safety and security of France's expansive territory (for the Navy). Deploying additional forces to Eastern Europe in significant numbers most likely would require removing assets from these missions, which might incur political resistance.

Conclusions and Implications for U.S. Policy

France could support a U.S.-led war in Eastern Europe; it has and is developing the capabilities required to take on a sophisticated peer and help meet some of the needs identified to participate in high-intensity conventional warfare. There also are a number of areas in which U.S.-French collaboration would make sense, among them electronic warfare, the challenge of countering massed precision fires, and air defenses. Specific modes of cooperation would have to be devised for each capability in ways that preserve the interests of both U.S. and French defense industry firms, but such cooperation can ensure that France addresses some of its challenges in fighting high-end conventional wars sooner than it would have otherwise.

Acknowledgments

We would like to thank key personnel of the project's sponsoring office, Leigh Nolan, Nina Wagner, and Brian Arakelian, for their support and guidance throughout this project. We would also like to thank the various individuals in France and the United States who took the time to share with us their insights, making an invaluable contribution to this report. Additional thanks go to Corentin Brustlein, Jean-Baptiste Jeangène Vilmer, Quentin Lopinot, Boris Toucas, and General (ret.) Olivier Tramond for helping facilitate conversations in France. We also thank Jim Dobbins from the RAND Corporation and Alice Pannier for their thoughtful reviews of an earlier draft of this report. Their comments were immensely helpful. Finally, we would like to thank our editor, Jessica Wolpert.

Abbreviations

2017 Strategic Review	2017 Defense and National Security Strategic Review
A2/AD	anti-access/area denial
ASMPA	Air-Sol Moyenne Portée
ASN4G	Air-Sol Nucléaire Fourth-Generation
CAESAR	Camion Équipé d'un Système d'Artillerie
CSO	Composante Spatiale Optique [Optical Space Component]
CUGE	Charge Universelle de Guerre Électronique
EU	European Union
EUROMALE	European Medium Altitude Long Endurance
FCAS	Future Combat Air System
FC/ASW	Future Cruise and Anti-Ship Weapon
FREMM	Frégate Européenne Multimission [European Multimission Frigate]
GDP	gross domestic product
ISR	intelligence, surveillance, and reconnaissance

LPM	Loi de Programmation Militaire [Military Programming Law]
MLRS	multiple launch rocket system
MRTT	multinational multirole tanker transport
NATO	North Atlantic Treaty Organization
SEAD	suppression of enemy air defenses
SSBN	ballistic missile submarine
UAV	unmanned aerial vehicle
VAB	Véhicule de l'Avant Blindé
VBCI	Véhicule Blindé de Combat d'Infanterie
VBL	Véhicule Blindé Léger

CHAPTER ONE

Introduction

The United States and France's history of military cooperation dates back to the American Revolutionary War.[1] Although the Macron presidency has been marked by a renewed effort to boost Europe's ability to address collective defense issues by giving it "autonomous operating capabilities,"[2] France has remained strongly committed to the North Atlantic Treaty Organization (NATO) and bilateral defense cooperation with the United States. French forces work closely with U.S. forces in Africa and the Levant, and the French have been participating in reassurance and deterrence efforts in northeastern Europe since 2014. Furthermore, France has reversed a two-decade trend of defense budget cuts; in the 2017 Defense and National Security Strategic Review (hereafter referred to as the 2017 Strategic Review), France clearly commits to reaching the NATO goal of 2 percent of gross domestic product (GDP) in defense spending by 2024.[3] Against this background, we seek to examine which military capabilities France might bring to a large-scale conventional war in a scenario that focuses on Europe as a theater of conflict and Russia as the aggressor. Does France have ade-

[1] For a reference to this "mighty alliance" (as described by U.S. President Donald Trump) and these "ancient bonds" (as described by French President Emmanuel Macron), see White House, "Remarks by President Trump and President Macron of France in Joint Press Conference," April 24, 2018.

[2] Emmanuel Macron, "Initiative for Europe," speech at the Sorbonne University, Paris, September 26, 2017.

[3] République Française, *Defense and National Security Strategic Review*, 2017a, p. 58, paragraph 192.

quate capabilities for such a fight, and if not, how likely is it to obtain them in the near future?

This case study of France has two purposes. First, we aim to examine France's current and future ability to share the burden with the United States and its other allies in the event of a large-scale conventional war against Russia. Second, we seek to provide recommendations to address potential capability gaps. This analysis is framed around the following key questions:

- To what extent is preparing for a large-scale conventional war a French priority? How does it compare with other contingencies?
- What is France's level of readiness for such a conflict, and what would France's comparative advantages be in this conflict?
- Which future programs (planned or potential) would be most likely to increase France's capabilities for a high-intensity conflict?
- Finally, which internal or external factors might constrain the development of France's military capabilities and its ability to use them in a European large-scale conventional war scenario?

To address these questions, we examined primary sources in French, such as official strategies, doctrinal documents, transcriptions of hearings before the French Parliament, and legislative documents. We also reviewed secondary sources in French and English on France's strategic priorities, military capabilities, and defense issues. Finally, we had more than a dozen conversations between March and May 2019 with French government officials, active-duty and retired French military officers, and French researchers specializing in defense issues.

We find that although France is not particularly concerned with a Russian conventional attack in Europe, which it believes to be highly unlikely, it is well aware of the damage that a resurgent Russia can cause in other regions, such as the Middle East and the North Atlantic, as well as in the hybrid domain. France's priority of maintaining *strategic autonomy*—which it defines as its ability to fight any war and to remain a nuclear power—has resulted in the maintenance of high-end conventional capabilities, even though it has mostly used low-end capabilities in its recent fights in Mali and the Central African Republic. The 2019–2025 Military Programming Law (Loi de Programmation Militaire, or LPM) puts a strong emphasis on modernizing some of the equipment that would be used in a large-scale, conventional contingency; improving the readiness of existing equipment; and boosting troops' morale and training. However, some gaps will remain beyond 2025 because France trades depth for breadth—France is able to conduct military operations across the full spectrum of conflict, but it does not have the ability to sustain the fight during a protracted conflict against a highly capable adversary, such as Russia. From a U.S. perspective, this means that France could participate in a large-scale conventional war in Eastern Europe for a limited time. Several capability areas, such as electronic warfare and air defenses, might benefit from increased U.S.-French collaboration and could improve France's ability to sustain this type of conflict.

Organization

We examine France's strategic priorities, focusing on its views on the burdensharing concept and its greatest security concerns, and also examine how these priorities broadly affect equipment and personnel decisions (Chapter Two). We then examine Army (Chapter Three), Air Force (Chapter Four), and Navy (Chapter Five) capabilities, focusing on equipment and personnel, readiness, and the broad priorities of the services for the near future. We also look at France's most recent and forthcoming space, cyber, and intelligence capabilities (Chapter Six). Finally, we discuss potential political, legal, and logistical obstacles to French participation in a combined operation to defeat aggression by Russia (Chapter Seven). In conclusion, we assess whether France could support a U.S.-led war effort in Eastern Europe and highlight capability areas with potential for increased U.S.-French collaboration.

CHAPTER TWO

Overview of France's Defense Approach

Key Principles of France's Strategy

France's strategic documents, as well as the defense decisions that were made over the previous decades, suggest that several key principles have guided, and continue to guide, France's doctrine, posture, and procurement decisions. Although these principles could be formulated in different ways, three stand out in particular: (1) France is a nuclear power and will remain so; (2) France should be able to intervene anytime, anywhere to protect its national interests; and (3) the French defense industry is a national interest and should be protected. These principles have been reaffirmed in the 2017 Strategic Review; they guide the LPM; and they were confirmed in our conversations. Nothing indicates that these principles will change in the future. The first two constitute the space within which France makes its defense-related decisions. Any policy or military option that would drastically violate one of these principles will likely be ignored or rejected. The third principle guides many French decisions, but it likely could be bypassed if the first two principles were challenged.

France Is a Nuclear Power and Will Remain So

Nuclear dissuasion has been a defining feature of France's strategic posture since 1954, when the French government, led at the time by Pierre Mendès-France, launched the first program to build nuclear weapons and submarines.[1] Then–President Charles de Gaulle made it clear in the late 1950s that France should have the ability to independently wage war—a decision that paralleled the French withdrawal from NATO's integrated command structure in 1966.[2] This position has not changed since.[3] The 2017 Strategic Review makes clear that this is still France's view today ("Nuclear deterrence remains the cornerstone of our defense strategy"[4]) and in the foreseeable future ("Maintaining our deterrent over the long term is essential"[5]). France's February 2019 simulation of a nuclear attack mission, complete with refueling and the launch of a missile on a test site, clearly aims to signal readiness in that domain.[6] In February 2020, President Emmanuel Macron stated that, if needed, a "nuclear warning" could be delivered to a state actor threatening France's vital interests to "reestablish deterrence."[7]

Accordingly, Macron has emphasized the modernization of France's nuclear deterrent, and the LPM commits $5.6 billion per year to this objective starting in 2020—an increase from approximately $4 billion a year.[8] The expected total investment to ensure the complete modernization of both the air and sea components of the French

---

1 Nicolas Roche, *Pourquoi la Dissuasion*, Paris: Presses Universitaires de France, 2017, p. 91.

2 Dominique Mongin, "Genèse de l'Armement Nucléaire Français," *Revue Historique des Armées*, No. 262, 2011, pp. 8–9.

3 Corentin Brustlein, "Forces Nucléaires Françaises, Quel Renouvellement?" *Politique Étrangère*, Vol. 3, 2017, p. ii; conversation with senior French defense official A, March 2019; conversation with former senior French defense official A, March 2019; conversation with senior French defense officials, March 2019.

4 République Française, 2017a, p. 69, paragraph 240.

5 République Française, 2017a, p. 70, paragraph 248.

6 Sebastian Sprenger, "French Air Force Rehearses a Long-Range Nuclear Strike," *Defense News*, February 5, 2019a; John Irish and Sophie Louet, "France Carries Out Rare Simulation of Nuclear Deterrent Strike," Reuters, February 5, 2019.

7 Translated from Élysée, "Discours du Président Emmanuel Macron sur la Stratégie de Défense et de Dissuasion Devant les Stagiaires de la 27ème Promotion de l'École de Guerre," February 7, 2020.

8 Brustlein, 2017, p. i; "La Coûteuse Modernisation de la Dissuasion Nucléaire," Agence France-Presse, June 21, 2018; République Française, 2017a, p. 6; Irish and Louet, 2019.

nuclear deterrent by 2035 will be 41.6 billion euros from 2019 through 2025, or more than 10 percent of all committed funds for defense.[9] France's modernization of its nuclear deterrent follows a long-established principle of strict sufficiency, meaning that France wants just enough nuclear assets to signal to potential enemies that it has the ability to inflict irreparable damage.[10]

A consequence of this nuclear focus is that France will be less capable of investing in conventional capabilities when faced with important deadlines for modernization of its nuclear military capabilities, unless—as is the case with the current LPM—it increases its overall defense budget. However, the focus on the nuclear deterrent also prioritizes some conventional assets.[11] For instance, the need to ensure the credibility of a potential nuclear strike was a driving factor in the decision to modernize the tanker aircraft fleet and acquire more multinational multirole tanker transports (MRTTs).[12]

France Should Be Able to Intervene Anytime, Anywhere to Protect Its National Interests

A second key principle guiding France's defense strategy is having the capacity to intervene militarily anytime and anywhere to protect French national interests. This principle closely parallels the first one and similarly originates with de Gaulle's decision in the late 1950s to ensure France's strategic autonomy. France sees itself as a middle power with a global reach. It has overseas departments and territories across the world, 2.2 million nationals living abroad, military bases in Africa and the Middle East, allies and partners on all continents, and a permanent seat at the United Nations Security Council that gives it a prominent position on global security issues.[13] Since the end of the

---

9 "La Coûteuse Modernisation de la Dissuasion Nucléaire," 2018.

10 Brustlein, 2017, pp. ii–v.

11 Conversation with senior French defense official B, March 2019; conversation with French researchers on defense issues, March 2019.

12 Conversation with former senior French defense official A, March 2019.

13 Boris Toucas, "Understanding the Implications of France's Strategic Review on Defense and National Security," Center for Strategic and International Studies, October 19, 2017.

Cold War, France's approach has been to maintain capabilities for the entire spectrum of conflict rather than specialize in low-intensity expeditionary warfare.[14] To address four types of contingencies—homeland security, "crisis in our neighborhood," "nonstate adversaries," and "military confrontation with state actors,"[15] the 2017 Strategic Review makes clear that "the required ability of our armed forces to operate across all domains and scenarios justifies maintaining a full-spectrum and balanced force model, as a prerequisite for our strategic autonomy," an ambition that was already mentioned in the two previous Strategic Reviews in 2008 and 2013.[16] Before being embraced by the European Union (EU),[17] the notion of strategic autonomy was thus a French one, and it is still at the core of the French defense policy.

This ambition of being able to intervene anywhere and anytime has several key implications. First, it compels France to invest in a number of domains in which insufficient capabilities, or dependence on others' capabilities, would jeopardize strategic autonomy. It also requires France to have some sophisticated capabilities in various domains in addition to its nuclear deterrent; these deterrents vary from command and control to intelligence and cyber.[18] France also is keen on being able to play the role of a "framework" nation in a coalition operation, which reinforces its interest in command and control capabilities.[19]

---

[14] In Europe, the United Kingdom is the only other country that has an approach similar to that of France. This commonality is at the basis of the Lancaster House Agreement, which ensures defense cooperation between both countries that will continue to exist past Brexit (conversation with senior French defense official B, March 2019; see also République Française, 2017a, p. 59, paragraph 197).

[15] République Française, 2017a, p. 51, paragraphs 150–153.

[16] République Française, 2017a, p. 51, paragraph 154.

[17] EU, *Shared Vision, Common Action: A Stronger Europe—A Global Strategy for the European Union's Foreign and Security Policy*, Brussels, June 2016, p. 5.

[18] Guillaume Lasconjarias and Florent de Saint Victor, "Chasing Grandeur? What You Need to Know About the 2017 French Strategic Review," *War on the Rocks*, October 27, 2017.

[19] République Française, 2017a, p. 73, paragraph 262, and p. 77, paragraph 285.

Second, France must have a military that covers the entire range of possible missions to ensure that it never completely depends on someone else's forces to respond to a given contingency[20]—which does not mean that it does not welcome allied support when it decides to intervene. France's ability to invest in dedicated means for specific contingencies is constrained by limited resources, and as a result the French military prefers multirole equipment that can be employed in a variety of missions. Examples include the new Multirole Armored Vehicle (Véhicule Blindé Multirôle), also known as the Griffon; the Rafale fighter aircraft; and the European Multimission Frigate (Frégate Européenne Multimission, or FREMM). Personnel training follows a similar course. French personnel in all three services train for the entire spectrum of contingencies, from irregular warfare to conventional missions.

A third implication is that the French armed forces lack depth, meaning that demanding operations would quickly exhaust both France's human and material resources.[21] The human resources problem is especially acute with respect to "generating force" and various combat support and combat service support formations, which were particularly targeted by post–Cold War cuts. A dearth of aircraft maintenance personnel, for example, has been one of the reasons cited for poor aircraft availability.[22] The lack of material resources can be seen in terms of not just France's relatively small number of specific types of weapon system but also its small amount of ammunition and spare parts. Additionally, the increased sophistication of military equipment means that the same amount of money buys fewer systems; when assets are replaced by newer versions, their numbers sometimes go down—for instance, France replaced its previous 155-mm howitzers with a smaller number of more-advanced Camion Équipé d'un Système d'Artillerie

---

20 Sénat, Hearing of Chief of the Joint Staff General François Lecointre on the 2019 Draft Budget Law, October 10, 2018c.

21 Conversation with senior French defense officials, March 2019; conversation with French researchers on defense issues, March 2019; conversation with senior French defense official C, March 2019.

22 Vincent Lamigeon, "56% des Aéronefs Incapables de Voler : L'Incroyable Talon d'Achille de l'Armée Française," *Challenges*, December 11, 2017.

(CAESAR) systems.[23] France's choice has been to maintain a full range of capabilities, even with very small numbers of assets. One rationale behind this choice is the notion that it is easier to increase an existing capability than to create one ex nihilo.[24]

The French military's willingness to maintain small inventories of weapon systems and ammunition might be strengthened by its excellence in operating remarkably lean expeditionary operations. The blessing (or curse) of the French military's knack for lean operations was on display in Operation Serval, which was conducted in Mali in 2013–2014. The entire mobilization effort was constrained by France's inability to do more than portion out its forces incrementally, bringing to bear, for instance, a few additional Rafales, a few CAESAR self-propelled howitzers, and a few helicopters, often without the logistics officers or even air traffic controllers required to manage the flow at the receiving end of the logistical chain. The scarcity of resources meant the French had to take risks. For example, the limited number of CAESARs and lack of various forms of support, including medical capacity, meant that Operation Serval commander General Bernard Barrera had on several occasions to opt for sequential operations rather than conduct them simultaneously[25]—an issue that more broadly raises questions regarding the ability of France to conduct larger-scale or more-intense warfare. When the French military experienced budget cuts, the remaining spending tended to focus on ongoing operations, which took place largely against adversaries using unconventional warfare. As a result, less attention was given to maintaining or acquiring conventional weapons.[26] In October 2018, Chief of the Joint Staff General François Lecointre stated before the Sénat that "[i]n 2025, [French] armed forces will be consolidated and modernized . . .

---

[23] Conversation with French researchers on defense issues, March 2019.

[24] Conversation with senior French defense officials, March 2019.

[25] Bernard Barrera, *Opération Serval: Notes de Guerre*, Mali 2013. Paris : Éditions du Seuil, 2015, pp. 161, 172, 177, 366.

[26] Conversation with French researchers on defense issues, March 2019.

but unable to face a major conflict such as a massive interstate war. This seems obvious to me."[27]

Other European countries have experienced this dilemma over whether to maintain capabilities for current operations or modernize for different types of contingencies. For example, the United Kingdom's participation in the wars in Iraq and Afghanistan has created a dominant land force, with the Royal Air Force and the Royal Navy's modernization programs lagging behind. Generally, the United Kingdom prioritizes equipment programs that serve low-intensity, expeditionary warfare.[28] Germany is attempting to turn toward a force that could continue out-of-area operations while undertaking more high-intensity tasks (including protecting the national territory) and projecting power around the globe. However, the cost of such ambitions might be more than what German domestic opinion can accept.[29]

As for France, the LPM tries to regain some of the ground that has been lost at the high end of the conflict spectrum and to somewhat rebalance capacities.[30] The LPM plans for French forces to be deployed in three concurrent theaters of operations, "including the ability to play the role of framework nation on one theater and to be a major contributor to a coalition."[31] What the LPM calls a "major engagement in intervention" will also receive more sea and air capabilities, as well as a cyber component. However, planning for a major engagement assumes

---

27 Sénat, 2018c.

28 Andrew Dorman, *The Future of British Defence Policy*, Institut Français de Relations Internationales, Focus Stratégique No. 74, July 2017, p. 25.

29 Sebastian Sprenger, "More Money, More Missions: German Defense Minister Unveils Her Plan for the Bundeswehr," *Defense News*, November 7, 2019b; Sebastian Sprenger, "Germany Unveils Growth Plan for the Bundeswehr," *Defense News*, September 5, 2018.

30 Conversation with senior French defense officials, March 2019.

31 Translation from Dominique de Legge, "Avis Présenté au Nom de la Commission des Finances Sur le Projet de Loi, Adopté par l'Assemblée Nationale Après Engagement de la Procédure Accélérée, Relative à la Programmation Militaire pour les Années 2019 à 2025 et Portant Diverses Dispositions Intéressant la Défense," *Sénat*, No. 430, May 15, 2018a, p. 20.

that France would conduct one as part of a coalition; in any case, the French military does not use Russia as a pacing threat.[32]

The French Defense Industry Is a National Interest and Should Be Protected

A third key principle guiding French defense strategy is maintaining France's defense industry, which is considered critical to ensure France's security. France's defense industry provided 6 billion euros in revenue in 2016 and represented 200,000 jobs in 2017.[33] Accordingly, the 2017 Strategic Review states that "Ensuring reliable procurement and support for our armed forces, particularly those with a role in nuclear deterrence, is a prerequisite for France's freedom of action, making this activity a pillar of its strategic autonomy."[34] This also requires a sustained pace of exports to maintain the viability of France's defense industrial base. To maintain the Rafale production capability, for instance, 11 new aircraft are needed per year; for the A400M, ten aircraft a year are necessary.[35]

France is therefore eager to support this industry and ensure that procurement is done on a national basis, particularly for the most-strategic items and those that allow France to maintain certain skills and technologies.[36] There is, in particular, reluctance to buy off-the-shelf equipment related to high-end or nuclear deterrence missions from others,[37] as France prefers to keep as much autonomy as possible in these domains. For instance, a French company—Thales—has been

---

[32] Lasconjarias and de Saint Victor, 2017; the United States serves as the French military's pacesetter because of France's interest in interoperating with U.S. forces as a respected partner (conversation with French researchers on defense issues, March 2019).

[33] République Française, 2017a, p. 63, paragraph 217.

[34] République Française, 2017a, p. 63, paragraph 218.

[35] de Legge, 2018a, p. 31.

[36] Jean-Dominique Merchet, "Chaudières et Catapultes: Les Enjeux Techniques du Prochain Porte-Avions," *Secret Défense*, January 27, 2017.

[37] Conversation with French researchers on defense issues, March 2019.

developing the new sonar system that will be used on nuclear-powered ballistic missile submarines.[38]

However, France cannot be self-sufficient in all domains and is engaged in a number of industrial cooperation projects. These often occur with European partners and usually are performed for the "least strategic" types of equipment.[39] The 2017 Strategic Review provides a list of defense capabilities that should be produced in a sovereign way (for instance, stealth vehicles or hardened core communications and networks),[40] those that can be produced "in cooperation with nationally preserved skills," those that can be produced "in cooperation with mutual dependency," and those that France will buy off the shelf.[41] France has resorted to off-the-shelf purchases for certain categories of equipment, such as airborne early warning and control systems, drones, missiles, and munitions.[42] For instance, France bought U.S.-made Javelin antitank missiles in 2010 in response to an urgent need in Afghanistan (although the French now are fielding a French-made replacement).[43] France similarly made an "emergency" purchase of MQ-9 Reaper drones in 2013 because it was beginning Operation Serval and lacked a French-made or even European-made equivalent. Since then, it has used these drones systematically, particularly in support of special forces operations.[44] Other examples of outside purchases

---

38 Allen Cone, "Thales to Develop Sonar System for New French Sub," UPI, February 8, 2018.

39 République Française, 2017a, p. 65, paragraph 227.

40 *Sovereign* is defined as "a purely national approach, that cannot be shared and where guarantees of hardware and software integrity, freedom of use, and operational superiority prevail" (République Française, 2017a, p. 65, paragraph 226).

41 République Française, 2017a, p. 65, paragraph 226.

42 Conversation with French researchers on defense issues, March 2019.

43 Pierre Tran, "France Receives Missiles, Launchers to Replace Milan Anti-Tank System," *Defense News*, November 30, 2017a.

44 Sénat, *Rapport d'information Fait au Nom de la Commission des Affaires Etrangères, de la Défense et des Forces Armées (1) Par le Groupe de Travail "Les Drones dans les Forces Armées,"* Paris, May 23, 2017b, p. 28.

include C-130 aircraft and GBU-12 Paveway guided bombs, which France is now using to arm its Reaper drones.[45]

France also joins asset pools to use assets that it does not produce. For instance, France does not make high-altitude, long-endurance unmanned aerial vehicles (UAVs) but joined the Alliance Ground Surveillance program with 14 other NATO nations to acquire five U.S.-made, NATO-operated Global Hawk systems.[46]

One important consideration that determines how quickly France can acquire new assets is the French defense industry's production pace. Increasingly sophisticated assets require longer production cycles, and the number of manufacturing facilities is limited (to only a single one in the case of submarines).[47] Exports, in particular, can limit France's ability to produce equipment for its own use, as they can monopolize production lines for years.[48] Another effect of France's sustained export policy has been to drive French armament industry research and development units toward the needs of the militaries that buy their products, rather than the French forces.[49] The equipment that France exports is unlikely to end up supporting, or complementing, France's assets in a multinational operation, as the large majority of French arms exports go to non-European and non-NATO nations.[50] Exports have also, at times, stretched thin France's military personnel (as they must train the buyers of the weapons) and its ability to restock its own equipment.[51]

---

45 Helen Chachaty, "Les Reaper Armés dès Fin 2019 à Niamey," *Le Journal de l'Aviation*, May 22, 2019.

46 NATO, "Alliance Ground Surveillance," updated June 21, 2019b.

47 Conversation with French researchers on defense issues, March 2019.

48 Conversation with French researchers on defense issues, March 2019.

49 Conversation with French researchers on defense issues, March 2019.

50 Conversation with French researchers on defense issues, March 2019. During 2014–2018, France's arms exports went primarily to the Middle East (44 percent), followed by Asia and Oceania (27 percent), far ahead of Europe (9.5 percent) (Stockholm International Peace Research Institute, *Trends in International Arms Transfers, 2018*, fact sheet, March 2019).

51 French Ministry of Armed Forces, as quoted in de Legge, 2018a, p. 25.

France's Approach to Burdensharing

The French are willing partners with respect to burdensharing.[52] They share with the United States the analysis of a strategic context increasingly marked by "the rise of international economic and military competition;"[53] a February 2019 speech by Macron described the "global competition between the United States and China" as "structuring [. . .] international relations" for the foreseeable future.[54] The French are committed to spending more on defense, and this translates relatively directly into warfighting and military deployments, as they are actively engaged in combat and other operations around the globe.

France generally can be counted upon to play a significant role in NATO or United Nations–flagged coalition operations—as they have in the Balkans, Afghanistan, and Libya—and it would likely participate in any Article 5 scenario. We also cannot overlook low-profile, but substantive, Franco-American military cooperation, especially as it relates to counterterrorism in the Sahel and the Horn of Africa. In the Sahel, in particular, France has demonstrated its willingness to put boots on the ground, and the United States has played a critical supporting role for the French troops there.

Commitment to Increased Defense Spending

French defense experienced what one analyst described as "chronic underfunding for nearly two decades,"[55] culminating in the resignation of Chief of the Joint Staff General Pierre de Villiers in July 2017 over Macron's initial decision to cut the 2018 defense budget by 850 mil-

[52] For a methodology to assess how much U.S. allies contribute to overall burdensharing, see King Mallory, Gene Germanovich, Jonathan William Welburn, and Troy D. Smith, *Burdensharing and Its Discontent: Understanding and Optimizing Allied Contributions to the Collective Defense*, Santa Monica, Calif.: RAND Corporation, 2020. Not available to the general public.

[53] Translation from de Legge, 2018a, p. 13. See also République Française, 2017a, p. 17, paragraph 2.

[54] Translated from Élysée, 2020.

[55] Brustlein, 2017, p. ii.

lion euros—a decision that he later reversed.[56] Defense spending eventually reached 34.4 billion euros in 2018, up from 32.6 billion euros in 2017.[57] 2019 saw an increase as well, to 35.9 billion euros,[58] and this rise is expected to continue in the next few years to reach 44 billion euros by 2023.[59] The French ministry of armed forces is planning on recruiting 21,600 military and 3,700 civilian personnel in 2019, a figure described as a "record" by Defense Minister Florence Parly.[60]

The defense budget's increase reflects an understanding that France's strategic environment is becoming more demanding; increasingly technologically complex military equipment requires more maintenance; cyber, space, and intelligence capabilities need dedicated investments; and some capability gaps need to be filled.[61] Some of the priorities identified for the next five years include intelligence, surveillance, and reconnaissance (ISR); transport aircraft; aerial refueling aircraft; maritime patrol aircraft; helicopters; and Army vehicles, as well as infrastructure for military families.[62] Another perceived need is to promote innovation within the military, and in September 2018, France created a joint Defense Innovation Agency (Agence d'Innovation de Defense), which it placed under the authority of the French defense procurement agency (Délégation Générale De l'Armement).[63] In 2019,

---

56 "Le Général de Villiers Revient sur Sa Démission Fracassante dans un Livre," Agence France-Presse, November 7, 2017.

57 Ministère des Armées, *2018 Defense Key Figures*, Paris, undated, p .7.

58 Sénat, Hearing of Defense Minister Florence Parly on the 2019 Draft Budget Law, October 15, 2018d.

59 de Legge, 2018a, p. 27. See also Janes, "Defense Budget Overview–France," September 27, 2018; Sophie Louet, "France Commits to Boosting Defense Spending by 35 Percent over Six Years," Reuters, February 8, 2018.

60 Sénat, 2018d.

61 Sénat, *2% du PIB: Les Moyens de la Défense Nationale*, May 2017a, pp. 1–2; conversation with senior French defense officials, March 2019.

62 Sénat, 2017a, p. 2.

63 Ministère des Armées, Direction Générale de l'Armement, "Création de l'Agence de l'Innovation de Defense et Nomination d'Emmanuel Chiva au Poste de Directeur," September 5, 2018.

France increased its budget for studies by 5 percent, to approximately $850 million, with an objective to reach $1.1 billion by 2022.[64]

A Renewed Effort Toward the 2-Percent Commitment

France's substantial defense budget increase represents an effort to get back to the annual 2 percent of GDP target that France exceeded until 2010 (see Figure 2.1). The 2017 French Strategic Review outlines the commitment of all European governments to reach this target by 2024.[65] This commitment was repeated by Parly in March 2019, as she stated in a speech in Washington, D.C., that "we fully support the U.S. insistence on the 2 percent."[66] She added that "President Macron has even suggested recently that the Europeans might enshrine this

Figure 2.1
French Defense Expenditures as a Percentage of GDP (2006–2018)

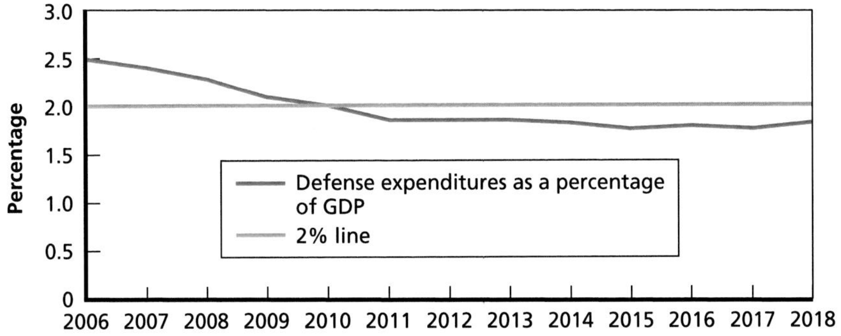

SOURCES: NATO, "Financial and Economic Data Relating to NATO Defense," press release, PR/CP(2011)027, March 10, 2011, Table 3, p. 6; NATO, "Defense Expenditures of NATO Countries (2011–2018)," press release, PR-CP(2019)034, March 14, 2019a, Table 3, p. 8.
NOTE: The share of real GDP percentage is based on 2000 prices (2006–2010 data) and 2010 prices (2011–2018 data). French figures for that time period do not change when calculated based on current prices rather than 2000 prices.

---

64 Sénat, 2018d.

65 République Française, 2017a, p. 58, paragraph 192.

66 Florence Parly, "The US-French Relationship in a Changing World," speech before the Atlantic Council, Washington, D.C., March 18, 2019a.

objective in a [t]reaty,"[67] a reference to Macron's call a few days earlier, in an editorial published in various European newspapers, for a European defense and security treaty that would be linked to NATO and commit Europeans to higher levels of defense spending.[68] To reach this 2-percent objective, however, the defense budget should reach about 50 billion euros by 2025, which will require an additional effort of 3 billion euros per year in 2024 and 2025 that is not explicitly covered in the LPM. More specifically, the LPM notes that the budgets for these two years will be set later, based on not just the 2-percent objective but also on France's economic situation at the time.[69] This opens the possibility that France's expenditure could remain below 2 percent by 2025 if economic indicators are not favorable.

The 2017 Strategic Review presents the 2-percent target as an opportunity for Europeans to take greater responsibility in their own security—a step made necessary, according to the review, by the "degradation of their strategic environment."[70] Burdensharing is conceived as a collective effort of Europeans that should allow them, in Parly's words, to "address their capability shortfalls, one by one."[71] In this "shortfalls" category, she includes "the key enablers: strategic transport, ISR, air tankers, cruise missiles," for which the United States provides 70 percent or more of the capabilities (up to 100 percent, in the case of strategic bombers and ballistic missile warning systems).[72] Burdensharing is therefore inseparable from the search for a greater ability of European nations to intervene where their interests are threatened, without depending on U.S. support to do so.[73] France's efforts toward

67 Parly, 2019a.

68 Victor Mallet and Mehreen Khan, "Macron Lays Out Proposals for a More 'Protective' EU," *Financial Times*, March 4, 2019.

69 de Legge, 2018a, p. 28.

70 République Française, 2017a, p. 58, paragraph 192.

71 Parly, 2019a.

72 Parly, 2019a.

73 In Parly's words, "We must grow the notion that a threat to our fellow Europeans is a threat to each of them, and that we need to step up and help, without waiting for the US to always foot the bill" (Parly, 2019a).

a European Intervention Initiative that would foster a common strategic culture among Europeans to facilitate, eventually, the conduct of joint interventions represent another move in that direction.[74] Parly described the European Intervention Initiative as "a useful initiative to bring some countries more distanced from so-called 'high end' operations than ours to share a common culture, through participation to recurrent exercises [and] joint thinking on the part of defense staffs."[75] France is still keen to reaffirm its strong commitment to NATO, and it calls for continued U.S. engagement in European affairs[76]—in other words, it welcomes burdensharing with the United States and is wary of burdenshifting on its part.[77]

French Participation in Operations

France also highlights, as a key element of its burdensharing, the fact that its contribution is, in Parly's words, a "war-fighting 2 percent" and "not a headquarter percentage;"[78] this percentage "all contributes to NATO security, whether in the Sahel, the Levant, or the North Atlantic, where our Navy cooperates with the [United States] to confront threats."[79] Even though French contributions are limited in number, France's capabilities partially make up for this limitation. An example is the French Army's contribution to the ground war against the Islamic State in Iraq and Syria. Apart from special forces, the French contingent consisted of only a few CAESAR howitzers and their crews. However, these crews were in high demand, thanks to their range and precision.[80]

---

74 Nick Witney, "Macron and the European Intervention Initiative: Erasmus for Soldiers?" European Council on Foreign Relations, May 22, 2018.

75 Translation from Sénat, 2018d.

76 Parly, 2019a.

77 Conversation with senior French defense officials, March 2019.

78 Center for Strategic and International Studies, "Global Leaders Forum: H.E. Florence Parly, Minister for the Armed Forces of France," video, YouTube, October 20, 2017.

79 Center for Strategic and International Studies, 2017.

80 Ministère des Armées, Opérations, "CHAMMAL: Task Force Wagram, 8 Mandats s'Illustrent dans la Lutte Contre Daech," May 3, 2019c; Olivier Fort, "Lessons Learned from

Parly also is referring to a French vision of burdensharing that focuses on a division of labor in which France conducts combat missions in other regions of the world, such as the Sahel, which are also of importance to NATO and the United States (not necessarily a renewed focus on Eastern Europe). Operation Barkhane can be viewed as such a burdensharing operation: French forces are combating Islamist groups in Africa's Sahel region that are affiliated with al Qaeda and the Islamic State. As of May 2020, there were 5,100 French troops deployed across Mali, Burkina Faso, Niger, and Chad as part of Operation Barkhane.[81] As of 2018, 64 percent of France's deployed forces were in the Sahel region (see Figure 2.2).

France is involved in several more theaters of operations, as well as with the France-based Operation Sentinelle, which was launched in January 2015 after the *Charlie Hebdo* attack and as of mid-2019 still had 7,000 soldiers mobilized (with an additional 3,000 reserves if needed).[82] Overall, France sustains a high tempo of operations that is equal or superior to the levels of deployment set in the 2013 White Paper on Defense and National Security.[83] This intensity of deployments has resulted in what a French senator described as "accelerated wear of equipment and an exhaustion of personnel."[84] Most of these deployments take place in areas where the United States is also deployed (see Figure 2.3). As of 2019, France and the United States were both involved in Iraq and Syria, the Sahel, and the Baltic States.[85]

CAESAR Deployment in Iraq," *Fort Sill Fires Bulletin*, September–October 2019.

[81] Ministère des Armées, Opérations, "Opération Barkhane," March 30, 2020.

[82] Ministère des Armées, Opérations, "Opération Sentinelle," undated.

[83] Brustlein, 2017, p. ii. Another source notes that "[t]he French military as a whole has maintained more than 10,000 personnel deployed simultaneously every year since the 1990s, with the army providing about 80 percent of these personnel" (Janes, "France—Army," October 1, 2018b).

[84] de Legge, 2018a, p. 16.

[85] France was involved with other partners in Lebanon (the United Nations Intermediary Force Lebanon), the Central African Republic (the United Nations Multidimensional Integrated Stabilization Mission in the Central African Republic and the European Union Training Mission), and the Mediterranean (French participation in EU Naval Force Mediterranean and Operation Sophia).

Figure 2.2
French Forces Deployed, by Foreign Theater of Operation (2018)

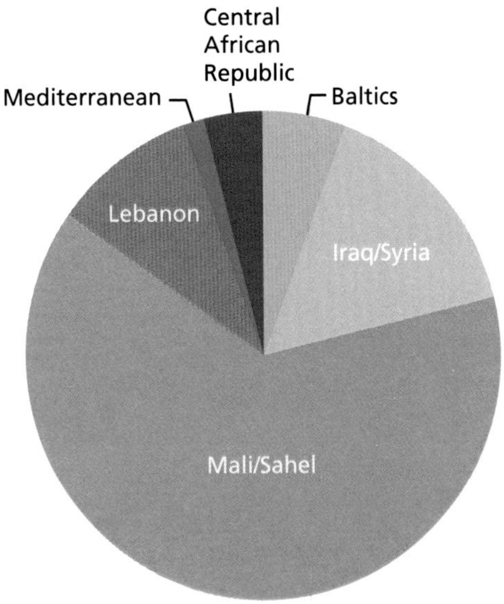

SOURCE: Ministère des Armées, Opérations, "Déploiements Opérationnels des Forces Armées Françaises," January 22, 2019a.

In July 2019, France, along with the United Kingdom, responded positively to increase by an estimated 10 to 15 percent the number of their special forces present on the ground in Syria.[86]

In Eastern Europe, France has participated in NATO's Baltic Air Policing since 2004 and its Enhanced Air Policing since 2018.[87] France has been contributing a company to the European Forward Presence in the Baltic States since March 2017 (Mission Lynx), first in the British-led battalion based in Estonia (2017), then in the German-led battalion in Lithuania (2017–2018) and, since May 2019, again with

---

[86] Lara Seligman, "Britain, France, Agree to Send Additional Troops to Syria," *Foreign Policy*, July 9, 2019.

[87] Ministère des Armées, Opérations, "EAP: Fin de Mandat pour l'Armée Française," August 30, 2018.

Figure 2.3
Number of French Troops Involved in Theaters of Operations

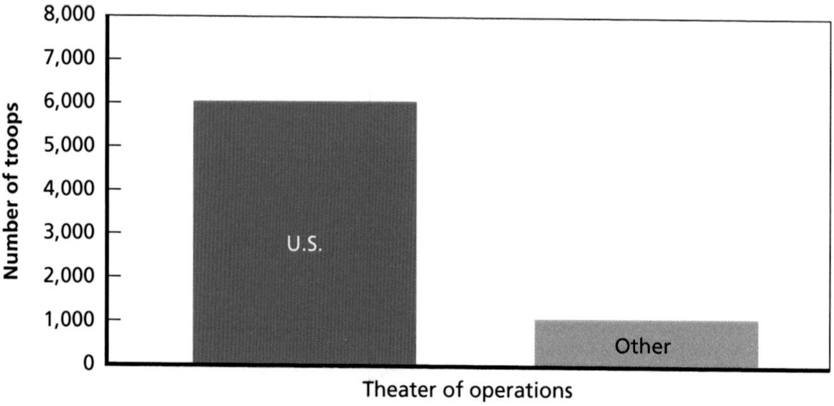

SOURCES: Ministère des Armées, Opérations, 2019a, except for the Central African Republic numbers (from Jane's Sentinel Security Assessment–Western Europe, "France-Army," October 1, 2018).
NOTE: Only includes deployments with more than 100 troops.

the Estonian-based, British-led battalion.[88] Operation Lynx mobilized 300 personnel,[89] as well as 13 state-of-the-art Véhicule Blindé de Combat d'Infanterie (VBCI) infantry fighting vehicles, four Leclerc tanks, four Véhicules de l'Avant Blindés (VAB) armored personnel carriers, and seven Véhicules Blindés Légers (VBL) light armored vehicles.[90]

France has also participated in a number of NATO exercises in the region, such as Steadfast Jazz in 2014, Citadel Bonus in 2017, and BALTOPS in 2019.[91] The NATO mission in northeastern Europe is politically important for France, as it provides an opportunity to show solidarity with European partners, affirms its place within NATO, and contributes to developing a privileged relationship with Baltic States.

---

[88] Ministère des Armées, Opérations, "Mission Lynx," August 28, 2019c, p. 3.

[89] Ministère des Armées, Opérations, 2019a.

[90] Ministère des Armées, Opérations, 2019c, p. 3.

[91] France, however, did not participate in Anakonda 16, possibly because French forces had to prioritize ongoing operations over exercises (Jean-Dominique Merchet, "Pologne: Les Militaires Français Ont du Mal à Regarder Vers l'Est," *L'Opinion*, June 12, 2016).

Estonia, for instance, sent an infantry unit, armored personnel carriers, and support elements to Operation Barkhane in 2018.[92]

Is Russia a French Strategic Priority?

The 2017 Strategic Review highlights various security threats originating in Russia, from a "permanent risk of escalation" in Ukraine[93] to "Moscow's aggressive posture" in the Baltics.[94] The review also describes Russia's increased operations in the north Atlantic as "a major concern"[95] and cites additional threats that are not specific to Russia but to which Russia contributes, such as

> at the upper end of the spectrum, the dissemination of large quantities of modern hardware (including the latest generation of tanks and attack helicopters, long range artillery and electronic warfare systems) [that] is challenging the balance previously favorable to European land forces, and may even reverse it in certain areas.[96]

In Eastern Europe, the review calls for "a set of measures to reaffirm [NATO's] unity and to respond with a balanced, deterrent, and predictable posture" that includes a Very High Readiness Joint Task Force and forward deployed forces.[97] However, a large-scale conventional war with Russia in that region is generally considered unlikely, for it would mean that deterrence—and particularly nuclear deterrence—

---

[92] Conversation with French researchers on defense issues, March 2019. Estonian Defense Minister Juri Luik explicitly linked Estonia's contribution to Operation Barkhane and France's participation to the Enhanced Forward Presence in Estonia ("Estonia to Contribute to French-Led Operation Barkhane in Mali," *Army Technology*, April 17, 2018.) See also Fergus Kelly, "Mali: Estonia Troops to Begin Operations in Gao," *Defense Post*, August 21, 2018.

[93] République Française, 2017a, p. 23, paragraph 40.

[94] République Française, 2017a, p. 23, paragraph 41.

[95] République Française, 2017a, p. 23, paragraph 42.

[96] République Française, 2017a, p. 48, paragraph 144. This concern also was voiced in a conversation with senior French defense officials, March 2019.

[97] République Française, 2017a, p. 23, paragraph 41.

had failed.[98] Officials we spoke with appeared confident that a confrontation in Eastern Europe between Russia and NATO would quickly escalate to nuclear threats and that Russia would not risk a nuclear war.[99]

The "French nuclear umbrella" extends beyond French borders, as then–French President François Hollande made clear in 2015 and the Strategic Review reaffirmed in 2017.[100] In 2020, Macron went further and mentioned the "authentically European dimension" of French nuclear forces.[101] He also offered France's European partners the possibility to take part in French nuclear forces exercises.[102] However, between the beginning of Russian aggression and the moment when the United States or France threatens to retaliate with nuclear force, NATO might request some conventional support on the part of France.[103] In that case, France would have to make some hard trade-offs between providing such a contribution and maintaining the nuclear deterrent, as some assets—fighter aircraft, refueling capacities, airborne early warning and control systems—would likely be needed for both missions.[104]

Hybrid, rather than conventional, attacks are perceived as a more likely scenario in northeastern Europe. Russia might try to destabilize its neighbors through disinformation or through support to paramilitary groups in an attempt to test and weaken NATO—a Donbass-like

---

98 Conversation with senior French defense official A, March 2019; conversation with senior French defense officials, March 2019.

99 Conversation with senior French defense official A, March 2019; conversation with senior French defense officials, March 2019.

100 "The definition of our vital interests cannot be restricted to the national scope, because France does not conceive its defense strategy in isolation, even in the nuclear field" (République Française, 2017a, p. 52, paragraph 159; Élysée, "Déclaration de M. François Hollande, Président de la République, sur la Dissuasion Nucléaire, à Istres le 19 février 2015," February 19, 2015).

101 Our translation from Élysée, 2020.

102 Élysée, 2020.

103 Conversation with French researchers on defense issues, March 2019.

104 Conversation with French researchers on defense issues, March 2019.

scenario is perceived as a more plausible threat than a Crimea-like scenario.[105] The French Joint Staff takes into consideration such destabilization scenarios in the Baltic States.[106]

France is also concerned with Russian threats to its south and southeast, particularly Russia's involvement in the war in Syria, its increased role in Libya, and its greater presence in the Mediterranean Sea (25 ships as of September 2018).[107] This Russian involvement creates opportunities for incidents and escalation.[108] During his hearing before the French Sénat in October 2018, Navy Chief of Staff Admiral Christophe Prazuck mentioned the September 2018 accidental targeting of a Russian aircraft by Syrian air defense, which could have hit the French ship *Auvergne* as collateral damage.[109] These concerns are shared across services. During a hearing before the Sénat in October 2018, Air Force Chief of Staff General Philippe Lavigne mentioned as a major concern the presence in Syria of ground-to-air defense systems and sophisticated Russian and Syrian fighter aircraft in close proximity to French aircraft, as well as the use of electronic warfare to "jam coalition drones, GPS-guided weapons, and aircraft armament and navigation systems."[110] Beyond Syria, Russia's use of sophisticated electronic warfare is perceived as particularly problematic, given France's investment in communication-heavy, collaborative combat systems that need to be resilient to function in contested environments.[111]

---

[105] Conversation with French researcher on defense issues, March 2019; conversation with French researchers on defense issues, March 2019.

[106] Conversation with French researcher on defense issues, March 2019.

[107] Sénat, Hearing of Navy Chief of Staff Admiral Christophe Prazuck on the 2019 Budget Draft Law, October 9, 2018b.

[108] Sénat, 2018b.

[109] Sénat, 2018b. See also Pierre Alonso, "Méditerranée: Chaotique Cohabitation Entre Marines Russe et Française," *Libération*, September 20, 2018.

[110] Sénat, Hearing of French Air Force Chief of Staff General Philippe Lavigne on the 2019 Draft Budget Law, October 24, 2018e.

[111] Conversation with French researchers on defense issues, March 2019.

CHAPTER THREE

Army Capabilities

The French Army, an all-volunteer force of 119,000 officers and soldiers (98,000 active and 19,000 reserves) is one of the most proficient ground forces in Western Europe.[1] It has a comprehensive range of capabilities and boasts considerable combat experience. It benefits from several years of growing budgets, a recruiting effort that has grown its deployable force, and a modernization program that is bringing the Army to the cutting edge of technology. This does not mean, however, that France is necessarily well suited for high-intensity conventional warfare. The French aim for a compromise position between the two ends of the conflict spectrum—what they call the segment médian (middle segment)—which they hope will be adequate for as broad a swath of the conflict spectrum as possible, even including conventional warfare. That said, their assessment of what is adequate is colored to some extent by their estimation of the low probability of a major war at the most extreme end (i.e., a war against Russia) and the assumption that if they were to get into a war with Russia, it would be as part of a coalition (and would be over quickly). Moreover, although the Army does train for conventional warfare, it spends most of its time engaged in conflicts at the lower end of the conflict scale.

Like all other European armies, the Army shed more than half its size following the end of the Cold War. In the 1970s and 1980s, it had approximately 300,000 soldiers—roughly half conscripts—

[1] Ministère des Armées, Armée de Terre, "Qui Sommes-Nous?" undated.

divided into three army corps and 15 divisions.[2] Today, it boasts about 119,000 active-duty troops—all volunteers—and two divisions. However, a relatively larger proportion of the Army is deployable because Army conscripts legally could not be deployed abroad, a restriction that limited France's capacity to contribute to the Gulf War. France's struggle to deploy about 16,000 troops to that war—a small number relative to the overall size of the force—reinvigorated the debate that led to the adoption of the all-volunteer force in 1996.[3]

The Army also is considerably smaller with respect to the number of major weapon systems. For example, in 1990, the French Army had 1,300 main battle tanks in service; today it has roughly 220.[4] Today's Leclercs are significantly more capable than 1990's AMX-30s, but the Army's capacity has nonetheless been reduced from two heavy armored divisions to two armored brigades.

A Turn Toward Networked Warfare

The Army has a balanced force structure that should serve it well in nearly all types of conflicts. Its 77,000 deployable forces are divided between two divisions and seven subordinate brigades (including the Franco-German Brigade), as well as a number of other combat support and combat sustainment support regiments, rotary-wing aviation, special operations units, and a NATO rapid reaction corps headquarters. Of the seven main brigades, two are heavy brigades, equipped with Leclerc main battle tanks, multiple launch rocket system (MLRS) batteries, and France's state-of-the-art VBCI infantry fighting vehicle; two are light, including France's one airborne brigade; and three are considered medium, or multirole. This translates into roughly enough

2 Jacques Chaumont, "Avis Présenté au Nom de la Commission des Affaires Etrangères, de la Défense et des Forces Armées, sur le Projet de Loi de Finances Pour 1981, Adopté par l'Assemblée Nationale," Paris: Sénat, November 19, 1980.

3 Ministère des Armées, Armée de Terre, "Opération Daguet: L'Armée de Terre dans la Guerre du Golfe," February 11, 2011.

4 Sénat, "Equipement de l'Armée Française en Chars de Combat—Sénat," 1990.

forces to be able to supply a battalion within a week and a brigade within a month.[5] Nearly all French units are mechanized: French doctrine places a high value on mobility. The French also possess amphibious capabilities, which are maintained by their Troupes de Marine (Marine) regiments.

The Army is now assuming the form it probably will keep for the next 20 years in both size and structure. The most important enhancement is the SCORPION modernization program. SCORPION represents the culmination of French Army investments in networked warfare that began in the 1990s, combined with a vehicle modernization program aimed at replacing a fleet of vintage light 1970s and 1980s vehicles and giving body to the French concept of the middle segment. At the heart of SCORPION is information and networking technology intended to network all the elements at various echelons, boost significantly the sharing of information, and facilitate logistics by automatically generating data regarding the condition and needs of deployed vehicles. At a tactical level, SCORPION enables collaborative warfare, a capability that presently only the Leclerc and the VBCI have.

Key to SCORPION's success will be the new Thales-built CONTACT radio and two information systems—the SCORPION Information and Combat System and the Système d'Information des Armées (Joint Information System). The SCORPION Information and Combat System is for use by regiments and smaller echelons; the Système d'Information des Armées is for the corps and division levels. At the same time, the French are rolling out the Griffon armored personnel carrier (first brought into service in July 2019) and the Jaguar light tank (expected in 2020). Both are designed to include the new networking and communications technology and will boast vetronics (the technology that monitors the vehicles and communicates data about the vehicles to facilitate logistics and sustainment).

CONTACT will be integrated with a Thales system called Antares. Antares will sit on the roof of the vehicles and provide "360-

---

[5] Michael Shurkin, *The Abilities of the British, French, and German Armies to Generate and Sustain Armored Brigades in the Baltics*, Santa Monica, Calif.: RAND Corporation, RR-1629-A, 2017, pp. 5–6, 10.

degree images around the vehicle" and can detect range-finding and targeting lasers pointed at it.[6] Antares ostensibly will be able to locate the source of the laser and identify, for example, whether it came from dismounted infantry, a tank, or some kind of aircraft. It will generate and present response options to the crew. Meanwhile, via CONTACT the system also will automatically share the data with everyone else present with the premise that either the system or others on the network will identify who is best placed to take a shot at the threat, if desired.[7]

France's Focus on the Middle Segment

The French insist on a one-size-fits all military, which they describe in terms of the middle segment. For the French, this means adding heavy assets back after post–Cold War cuts that disproportionately targeted France's heaviest assets—specifically, those parts of the Army designed to fight the Warsaw Pact in Germany. The French hope to design a force light enough for Mali yet heavy enough for most of the rest of the conflict spectrum. During the Cold War, France effectively maintained two separate armies: a large, conscription-based continental force designed to defend against the Warsaw Pact and a small, professional expeditionary force. Today Paris is motivated by the conviction that it cannot afford specialization and must instead invest in a small, but high-quality, professional one-size-fits-all force.

The tension the French feel between preparing for probable conflicts, such as in Africa, and for low-probability but high-risk encounters, such as a war against a peer, is common to other allies who participate in out-of-area deployments that tend to be relatively low intensity, such as peacekeeping missions. Most, if not all, NATO allies, for example, have deployed troops to Afghanistan, the Balkans, or any number

---

[6] Olivier Hertel, "14 Juillet: Le Griffon, Nouveau Blindé High-Tech de l'Armée de Terre," *Sciences et Avenir,* July 14, 2017.

[7] Hertel, 2017; Andrew White, "Thales Readies Antares for French Army," *Janes International Defence Review,* February 14, 2018.

of United Nations missions. The French, however, are distinguished by the frequency with which they undertake such missions, creating a need for capacity, as well as capability. French interests in Africa, moreover, make the need to be able to deploy to and operate in that theater necessary. It is all the more noteworthy, then, that the French have not opted for a primarily light force or even for a large, low-tech force, as recommended by some French military analysts. Some smaller NATO militaries have done that: Canada and the Netherlands, for example, backed away from conventional warfighting and such capabilities as main battle tanks in favor of lighter forces geared for coalition peacekeeping operations. France, in contrast, is striving to do it all.

France's move to the middle means, among other things, all but abandoning tracked vehicles while using heavier vehicles to replace the aging armored vehicle fleet that has been the mainstay of its expeditionary operations since the 1980s. Wheeled vehicles are easier to sustain and preferable for traveling long distances on their own power. This proved valuable in 2013 during Operation Serval, which obliged French armored vehicles to travel long distances by road to reach Mali and then operate in Mali. Currently, the only tracked vehicles in the Army's inventory are the Leclerc main battle tank, the U.S.-made MLRS, and AMX-30 AuF1 self-propelled howitzers from the 1970s (slated to be replaced by wheeled CAESARs, which feature conventional truck chassis). France recently retired the tracked 1970s-era AMX-10p infantry fighting vehicle, replacing it with the eight-wheeled VBCI.

The VBCI, however, is also significantly heavier than the AMX-10. The Griffon, which replaces the VAB armored personnel carrier, and the Jaguar, which replaces the AMX-10rc and the ERC-90 Sagaie light reconnaissance tanks, likewise are significantly heavier than their predecessors (see Table 3.1).[8] The weight bespeaks significant improvements in their survivability.

---

[8] The Griffon and Jaguar also boast a smaller cannon than their predecessors, relying on the new Missile Moyenne Portée antitank guided missile for when the 25-mm autocannon on the VBCI or the 40-mm gun on the Jaguar are insufficient. The AMX-10RC and ERC-90 had 105-mm and 90-mm guns, respectively.

Table 3.1
New French Armored Vehicles and Their Predecessors

New Vehicle	Entry in Service	Weight (tons)	Predecessor Vehicle	Entry in Service	Weight (tons)
Griffon	2018	20–24	VAB	1976	13.8
Jaguar	2020	20	AMX-10RC	1981	16
VBCI	2008	24–28	AMX-10P	1973	14
CAESAR	2003	15.9	AUF1	1977	42

SOURCES: "AMX-10P Infantry Fighting Vehicle," *Military Today*, undated; Ministère des Armées, Armée de Terre, "Canon 155 AUF1," July 13, 2016; Ministère des Armées, Armée de Terre, "VBCI—Véhicule Blindé de Combat de l'Infanterie," July 12, 2017; Ministère des Armées, Armée de Terre, "AMX 10 RC Renové," October 25, 2018; Ministère des Armées, Armée de Terre, "JAGUAR," January 30, 2019a; Ministère des Armées, Armée de Terre, "GRIFFON," July 15, 2019b; Ministère des Armées, Armée de Terre, "CAESAR," January 28, 2020.

The enhanced survivability and the advanced communications and networking technology the French are building into these vehicles make them more capable than needed for Africa. The older vehicles that were staples of French interventions in Africa in the 1980s through the 2000s, and are still to be found in French overseas operations today, appear to be deficient only in their reliability, which is a function of their advanced age. In other words, the French are not tailoring their force for low-intensity operations, even while they take care to ensure that it still is useful for such missions. The flip side of the coin is that the French are not optimizing their force for high-intensity conventional warfare either, for fear that such a force would be too difficult to deploy to and sustain in places like northern Mali. They are aiming for a force that would be "good enough" for both types of conflict.

Informing the Army's calculus is the conviction that a war at the highest end of the spectrum, something that might only be conceivable against Russia or China, is implausible because of nuclear weapons. Thus, their target for "good enough" arguably falls just below fighting Russians. The French also calculate that if they were to fight the Russians, it would be as part of a coalition. In any case, the risk of coming up short against Russia is a risk the French feel they have to take, given their need to build a force that can also be sent to the Sahel.

It is also worth noting that the overall numbers of the French Army's weapon system inventories are small. According to one source, the total number of large artillery pieces is 358 tubes, of which 121 are 155-mm tubes. Among those, 77 are state-of-the-art CAESARs and 32 are the 1980s-era AUF1. France has 140 120-mm mortars and only 13 MLRSs. The LPM calls for buying 32 more CAESARs, but the intent appears to be for them to replace the remaining AUF1 rather than raise the total number of self-propelled howitzers.[9]

The Challenge of Maintaining Readiness for High-Intensity Conventional Warfare

Up-to-date data regarding French readiness are hard to find. The available evidence indicates that in the 2000s, readiness suffered from budget cuts and reached a nadir during the 2014–2017 period while France was sustaining Operation Barkhane in the Sahel. Operation Sangaris in the Central African Republic, as well as Operation Sentinelle in the homeland, brought the force to a breaking point and convinced the government, with popular support, to start increasing the Army's budget and even grow the force by recruiting an additional 11,000, bringing the number of deployable troops from 66,000 to 77,000. At the same time, France also decided to breathe new life into its reserve system. The net result has been a revived force.

The improvement has been the most tangible with respect to soldiers and their training. More soldiers have made it possible to restore training levels to pre-2015 levels. Army Chief General Jean-Pierre Bosser made this clear in testimony given to the French National Assembly in 2017:

> With regard to readiness, the massive engagement on the national territory meant for the Army a drop in training that can be measured two ways. For one thing, the number of soldiers spending more than 150 days away from their garrison reached 16,000 in

[9] F. de St V, "L'artillerie Française—(Quelques Possibles) Tendances pour Demain en Operations 3/3," *Mars Attaque*, July 16, 2018.

> 2016. Also, the number of days dedicated to training dropped from 84 in 2014 to 64 in 2015, before climbing up to 72 in 2016. Adding 11,000 additional men restored our operational capital. My objective is to reach in the summer of 2018 the level that we had before the [terrorist] attacks of 2015.[10]

Significantly, Bosser indicated that it was specifically combined arms training that had been cut back, something he hoped to rectify so that he could deploy all the forces of the Army "to theaters of high intensity operations."[11] He also noted that equipment readiness was holding back the kind of training he wanted the Army to increase: "One can't have readiness for a combined arms group that includes a hard core of infantry or cavalry as well as engineers and artillery and logistical services unless the equipment is available."[12]

Bosser's comments and subsequent comments by several French officers indicate that the Army believes that the improved training regimen has at least restored the conventional warfighting skills it possessed prior to 2015.[13] What is less certain is how good the Army was at conventional warfighting before 2015. On paper at least, the Army knows how to fight conventional battles; officers attending France's equivalent to the Command and General Staff College, the Ecole de Guerre-Terre, focus on learning how to perform large-scale conventional operations. However, even if staff rides encourage officers to think about French battles in World War II, outside school, a French officer's world likely is defined by Operations Sentinelle and Barkhane (and, before those operations, Afghanistan).

The deployment in the Baltic States provides some on-the-ground training—particularly training in cold conditions—to units, including

---

[10] Translation from Commission de la Défense Nationale et des Forces Armées, Assemblée Nationale, "Audition du Général Jean-Pierre Bosser, Chef D'état-Major de l'Armée de Terre, sur le Projet de Loi de Finances pour 2018," October 11, 2017.

[11] Translation from Commission de la Défense Nationale et des Forces Armées, Assemblée Nationale, 2017.

[12] Translation from Commission de la Défense Nationale et des Forces Armées, Assemblée Nationale, 2017.

[13] Commission de la Défense Nationale et des Forces Armées, Assemblée Nationale, 2017.

one heavy unit that could not be employed for Operation Barkhane.[14] For some units previously included in Operation Sentinelle, the Baltic States are perceived as a more exciting operating environment that France itself.[15] The sieges of Mosul and Raqqa (Iraq) in Operation Chammal provided some artillery training; the French gunners used their CAESARs far more intensively and for a wider range of missions than they had in Afghanistan or the Sahel.[16] The artillery mission was also useful because French personnel were integrated into U.S. units, which proved highly beneficial for interoperability.[17] The conditions, however, were different from those of a large-scale conventional war in Europe because the French were not facing any sort of commensurate threat.[18]

With respect to major weapon systems, the situation is hardly positive, although reportedly improving. One basic problem is that even though the Army has more soldiers now, the amount of equipment has remained the same.[19] Increased spending is starting to help, but the issues created by the cost-cutting measures of the past decades largely remain. The Army, for example, has skimped on the purchase of spare parts, delegated maintenance work to manufacturers, and established a centralized rotational equipment scheme that reduced the overall size of vehicle fleets.[20] The scheme works by centralizing maintenance and providing vehicles to units only when and where they need them, as opposed to each unit possessing its own complete vehicle set and maintenance capabilities.[21] It is geared to operate in a lean fashion—possibly too lean, in light of the strain evident with respect to the effort to meet

---

14 Conversation with French researchers on defense issues, March 2019.

15 Conversation with French researchers on defense issues, March 2019.

16 Conversation with former senior French defense official A, March 2019; Florian Bunoust-Becques, "Du Sahel au Levant: Quelle Place pour l'Artillerie Française?" *Opérationnels—Soutien, Logistique, Défense, Sécurité*, January 8, 2019.

17 Conversation with former senior French defense official A, March 2019.

18 Conversation with former senior French defense official A, March 2019.

19 Commission de la Défense Nationale et des Forces Armées, Assemblée Nationale, 2017.

20 Commission de la Défense Nationale et des Forces Armées, Assemblée Nationale, 2017.

21 Commission de la Défense Nationale et des Forces Armées, Assemblée Nationale, 2017.

the requirements of mobilization for Operation Serval and the steady demands of Operations Barkhane and Sentinelle. Finally, the extreme conditions of the Sahel wear out equipment at a rate far greater than almost any other theater. Still, the data suggest some improvement from 2016 to 2017, and it is safe to assume increased gains through 2018 and 2019 (see Table 3.2).

Helicopters reportedly represent the most pressing issue. According to a 2018 Sénat report, only one out of every three helicopters in the French military (all services) was operable.[22] Roughly another third were being repaired or waiting for repair (pending the availability of hands to do the repair work or the requisite parts); the last third were

Table 3.2
Reported French Army Vehicle Availability in 2016 and 2017

Type	Number in December 2016	Percentage Available	Number in December 2017	Percentage Available
AMX-10 RC	249	48	247	57
GBC 180	5,282	60	5,229	64
Leclerc	241	61	243	64
VBCI	625	74	625	70
120-mm mortar	171	51	191	55
CAESAR	77	68	77	72
Petit Véhicule Protégé	1,176	31	1,176	43
VAB	2,475	42	2,651	46
TRM 700/100	116	35	112	30

SOURCE: Ministère des Armées, "Question No. 4412 de M. François Carnut-Gentille au Ministère des Armées," January 9, 2018a.
NOTES: The AMX-10 RC is a light tank. The GBC 180 is a basic heavy cargo truck. The Petit Véhicule Protégé is a light armored car. The VAB is an armored personnel carrier. The TRM 700/100 is a heavy equipment transporter.

---

[22] Dominique de Legge, "Le Parc d'Hélicoptères des Armées: Une Envolée des Coûts de Maintenance, Une Indisponibilité Chronique, des Efforts Qui Doivent Être Prolongés," *Sénat*, July 11, 2018b.

being worked on by manufacturers.[23] The low readiness rate is particularly serious, given the relatively small overall number of airframes in the French military's possession. The Army's parsimoniousness with its Tigre attack helicopters, for example, meant that none was available to French special forces operating in the Sahel, who had to rely on considerably less-powerful and more-vulnerable Gazelle helicopters for light attack duty;[24] the pilot of one Gazelle was killed by groundfire on the first day of the intervention in Mali.

A few press reports also point to ammunition shortages. MLRS rocket stocks, for example, are sufficiently scarce as to limit their deployment, according to one source, who also indicated that Hellfire missiles were in short supply.[25] The CAESARs deployed to Iraq as part of the anti–Islamic State of Iraq and Syria Task Force Wagram reportedly have been burning through worrisomely large numbers of shells and howitzer tubes because of the overuse of the small battery (four howitzers) and the extended ranges at which they have been firing.[26]

With regard to artillery acquisition, French plans suggest a focus on the lower end, rather than the high end, of the spectrum. The LPM plans for a larger number of 155-mm self-propelled howitzer CAESARs, the characteristics of which make it well-suited for expeditionary warfare but of debatable value in a conventional fight: It is unarmored and mounted on a wheeled conventional truck chassis. The CAESAR replaces the Cold War–era AUF-1, the tracks and armor of which make it much better suited for high-intensity warfare than expeditionary operations. The LPM does not plan to increase the number of MLRSs, which would be of tremendous value against a high-end adversary.[27]

---

23 de Legge, 2018b.

24 Jean-Christophe Notin, *La Guerre de la France au Mali*, Paris: Tallandier, 2014, p. 183.

25 Nathalie Guibert, "La Gestion des Munitions, un Sujet de Tension pour l'Armée Française," *Le Monde*, November 4, 2016.

26 Guibert, 2016; conversation with senior French defense official C, March 2019. A news report from September 2017 said that in one year the four CAESARs had fired 10,000 shells. See Laurent Lagneau, "Irak: En un An, l'Artillerie Française a Tiré Plus de 10.000 Obus Contre les Positions de l'État Islamique," *Zone Militaire*, September 22, 2017b.

27 Conversation with French researchers on defense issues, March 2019.

Enabling Mobility

France's busy expeditionary schedule obliges the Army to maintain its logistical abilities and its ability to move needed people and other resources. Two questions remain: (1) the resiliency of a lean system in the face of a conflict that is sure to require much greater resources and (2) whether France's ability to get what it needs where it needs to go can meet the requirements of a potentially much larger conflict. According to a senior flag officer, the system is resilient and France is able to get resources in place for a larger conflict, with the major caveat that France could not sustain such a fight for long. According to him, France's logistical capabilities and its capacity to move needed resources by rail are advantages. The French military, he explained, has maintained its close Cold War–era cooperation with the French rail service, the Société Nationale des Chemins de Fer Français, with the result that both the military and the rail service have retained the institutional knowledge and apparently the rolling stock required to ship materials not only within France but also from French and Spanish bases into and through Germany. Critically, this includes the ability to move items from French ports of entry on the Atlantic coast and the English Channel (which would be used by British and U.S. forces). Among other things, the French military has retained the legal authority to shut down rail (and air) traffic to make way for military convoys. According to the flag officer, France did this in 2013 during the scramble to project men and materiel to Mali and in 2019 in the rush to get the crew of the aircraft carrier *Charles de Gaulle* to port in time for its scheduled first voyage after a lengthy refitting.

On the negative side, however, is the thinness of the French military's human resources (the result of successive post–Cold War cuts to the generating force) and materiel shortages, such as those mentioned above. There are only so many vehicles, parts for those vehicles, and people with the necessary logistical skills to get those vehicles and parts where they need to go.

CHAPTER FOUR

Air Force Capabilities

The French Air Force, like France's other services, is significantly smaller than it was at the height of the Cold War, although it now has significantly more-powerful aircraft. It has gone from about 92,000 personnel (about a third of whom were conscripts) and 350 combat aircraft in 1990 to 40,000 volunteers and 217 fighter aircraft today.[1] In 2002, France began to improve its fleet with the introduction of Rafales and the retirement of Jaguars and various Mirage models. In recent years, the Air Force has been committed to further modernization. As of early 2019, the Air Force had two key priorities to maintain its ability to conduct full-spectrum operations. One is continuing to modernize its equipment, including preparing for the next generation of air combat system. The other is improving the Air Force's readiness in light of major shortcomings that were exposed during 2017–2018.

Modernizing Air Assets

France's Air Force modernization largely focuses on what Air Force Chief of Staff General Lavigne calls the "nuclear triptych" of fighter aircraft, missiles, and refueling aircraft.[2] Since 2008, the Rafale has

1 Armée de l'Air, "L'Armée de l'Air en Chiffres 2019–2020," April 21, 2020; Albert Voilquin, "Rapport d'Information fait au Nom de la Commission des Affaires Étrangères, de la Défense et des Forces Armées (1) en Application de l'Article 22, premier alinéa, du Règlement, sur la force aérienne tactique (F.A.T.A.C)," Sénat, October 10, 1990.

2 Sénat, 2018e.

gradually replaced the Mirage 2000N for the air component of the nuclear deterrent. This replacement was finalized in June 2018, when the last Mirage 2000N retired.[3] The Rafale is currently undergoing retrofitting to the F3R standard, which allows it to carry the METEOR long-range missile.[4]

One limitation to the pace at which France can acquire new assets is its defense industry's ability to keep up, particularly when commitments have already been made to exports that can monopolize production lines for years. For the Rafale, for instance, France received three new aircraft in 2018, but Dassault will only produce for exports (for contracts passed with Egypt, Qatar, and India) from 2019 to 2021, before producing another 28 aircraft for France between 2022 and 2024.[5] In 2023, France has planned to order another 30 Rafales, which it should receive between 2027 and 2030.[6]

Parly announced in January 2019 that 1.9 billion euros would be dedicated to the development of the F4 standard for the Rafale. This new standard, which is expected by 2027, will allow the Rafale to communicate better with other aircraft and ground assets.[7] F4 Rafales should also be able to carry heavier payloads, including new generations of precision guided munitions. Finally, they will have improved radar and jamming capabilities.[8] In terms of interoperability, the Rafales are interoperable with the Link 16 standard. The question of interoperability with the F-35 is still open, however, and discussions with the United States to reach that objective are only starting.[9] In the meantime, France remains engaged in the Trilateral Strategic Initiative with

---

3 "La Coûteuse Modernisation de la Dissuasion Nucléaire," 2018.

4 Conversation with senior French defense official D, April 2019. See also Laurent Lagneau, "La Direction Générale de l'Armement a Prononcé la Qualification du Standard F3-R du Rafale," *Zone Militaire*, November 9, 2018d.

5 Marie Dancer, "Nouvelle Commande Française pour le Rafale, Qui Poursuit sa Modernisation," *La Croix*, January 14, 2019.

6 Dancer, 2019.

7 Dancer, 2019.

8 Dancer, 2019.

9 Conversation with senior French defense official D, April 2019.

the United States and the United Kingdom; since its inception in 2013, the initiative has focused on the promotion of dialogue and interoperability between the three countries' air forces.[10] An F5 standard for the Rafale is expected by 2032, with high-speed communications enabled by a new Syracuse satellite and connected munitions.[11]

France plans to replace the Rafale with a sixth-generation aircraft by 2035–2040; in June 2019, the defense ministers of France, Germany, and Spain signed a framework agreement for the development of the Future Combat Air System (FCAS) that will fulfill that role.[12] Although it was still a concept in development, the FCAS should associate new fighter aircraft, cruise missiles, and drones and connect them to satellites, ground-based radars, NATO systems, and other combat systems on land and at sea.[13] France is taking the lead in developing the New Generation Fighter, while Germany will lead the development of the European Medium Altitude Long Endurance (EUROMALE) drone project, as well as the Maritime Patrol Systems 2030.[14] While the EUROMALE project is in development, France is adding six new REAPER drones to its fleet.[15] Overall, by 2025, France's drone capacity is expected to double from what it was in 2018.[16]

Tankers and strategic airlift are both relative weaknesses for France, owing largely to the age of its small tanker fleet and its lack of large cargo haulers comparable with the C-17. France often relies on U.S.-provided tankers to help meet its requirements in the Sahel. As for cargo, during Operation Serval, France had to turn to two com-

---

10 Sénat, 2018e. See also Peter Goldfein and André Adamson, "The Trilateral Strategic Initiative: A Primer for Developing Future Airpower Cooperation," *Air Force Journal of European, Middle Eastern, and African Affairs*, Spring 2019.

11 Conversation with senior French defense official D, April 2019.

12 Camille Brunier, "[Bourget 2019] Le SCAF Se Dévoile, des Annonces Importantes dans l'Aéronautique et le Spatial Militaire," *Ministère des Armées*, June 18, 2019.

13 Giovanni de Briganti, "Airbus, Dassault Jointly Awarded Two-Year SCAF/FCAS Architecture Study," *Defense-Aerospace*, February 5, 2019; Dancer, 2019.

14 de Briganti, 2019.

15 Conversation with senior French defense official D, April 2019; Sénat, 2018e.

16 Sénat, 2018e.

mercial operators of the massive Antonov and Ilyushin planes; one of these operators is part of the Russian Ministry of Defense.[17] The Russian heavy transporters reportedly carried fully 76 percent of Operation Serval's air cargo by volume.[18] France is replacing its fleet of aging C-135 and KC-135 tankers, as well as its A310 and A340 strategic troop and transport aircraft, with the A330 MRTT Phénix, which is both a tanker and a transport/cargo plane.[19] This replacement is happening faster than anticipated, with a decision made in September 2018 to have 12 of the 15 aircraft delivered as early as 2023 instead of in 2025.[20] By 2025, France expects to increase its transport capacity by 70 percent.[21] In addition, as of 2019, France and Germany were in the process of setting up a joint transport squadron with C-130 Hercules aircraft in 2019.[22] However, none of these improvements makes up for the absence of heavy lifters in the French fleet; the MRTT can carry up to 45 tons of cargo, according to Airbus, only about half that of the larger C-17. France will remain dependent on strategic lift provided by allies or foreign companies more broadly. Table 4.1 provides the numbers for additional items planned by 2025, as well as France's ambitions for 2030.

France is also modernizing its air-delivered munitions, including its medium-range air-to-ground nuclear missile, the Air-Sol Moyenne Portée (ASMPA). This program is expected to be completed by 2020, and an entirely new system (Air-Sol Nucléaire Fourth-Generation, or ASN4G) should replace the ASMPA by 2035.[23] The LPM plans for a new METEOR missile, as well as studies for a new interception, combat, and self-defense missile (known by its French acronym,

---

[17] Notin, 2014, p. 228.

[18] Notin, 2014, p. 236.

[19] Pierre Tran, "France Wants to Buy Airbus Tankers Sooner," *Defense News*, September 21, 2018b; Philippe Chapleau, "MRTT: Florence Parly Accélère la Livraison de 12 Avions Dont le Premier Sera à Istres Mi-Octobre," *Lignes de Défense*, *Ouest-France*, September 20, 2018.

[20] Tran, 2018b; Chapleau, 2018.

[21] Sénat, 2018e.

[22] Sénat, 2018e.

[23] "La Coûteuse Modernisation de la Dissuasion Nucléaire," 2018.

Table 4.1
Expected Increase in Number of Selected Main Systems by 2025 (Air Force)

System	Number as of 2019	Expected Number in 2025	Ambition in 2030
Reconfigured Tigre helicopters (from protection support to destruction support)	32	67	67
Rafale aircraft	143	171	225
Retrofitted M2000D	0	55	55
A 400M	14	25	53 tactical transport aircraft (A400M + C130J)
C130J	2	4	
MRTT	1	12	15

SOURCE: Adapted from de Legge, 2018a, p. 59.

MICA).[24] In addition, France and the United Kingdom are jointly developing the Future Cruise and Anti-Ship Weapon (FC/ASW), an air-launched cruise missile that will eventually replace the Exocet and SCALP-EG/Storm Shadow missiles.[25]

Hypersonic weapons represent a key issue of interest for the Air Force.[26] In January 2019, Parly announced that France would launch the V-MaX (Experimental Maneuvering Vehicle) project to equip French forces with a hypersonic glider.[27] With this program, France becomes the fourth country after the United States, Russia, and China to develop such weapons.[28] It is expected that the system will be used with the upcoming air-to-surface ASN4G missile, but the French government admitted that "the first use will probably not be for sev-

---

24 Sénat, 2018e.

25 Conversation with senior French defense official D, April 2019.

26 Conversation with senior French defense official B, March 2019.

27 "Race for Hypersonic Weapons Heats Up as France Joins 'Stealth by Speed' Contest," Agence France-Presse, January 29, 2019.

28 "France Joins Race to Develop "Hypersonic" Weapons, After China, Russia and US," Agence France-Presse, January 29, 2019.

eral years, and will be limited in terms of payload, flight time, and precision."[29]

Another system of note is the Charge Universelle de Guerre Électronique (CUGE) program for electronic warfare, which is also underway; according to Parly, as of June 2019, this program was arriving at its "final stage."[30] CUGE will equip three Falcon aircraft that will replace the current two Transall C-160 Gabriel aircraft tasked with signals intelligence gathering.[31]

Improving Equipment Readiness

Since 2017, France's defense ministry has devoted substantial efforts to improving the readiness of its military aircraft, which a November 2017 report found to have an availability rate of only 44 percent from 2012 through 2017.[32] Parly described this issue as the "Achilles heel" of the French armed forces.[33] The situation was particularly critical for some types of equipment, such as Caracal helicopters, more than 75 percent of which were not considered available for missions in late 2017.[34] This issue affected all three services, with mediocre readiness of the Tigre, Cougar, Puma, and NH90 TTH helicopters, in addition to the Caracal, for the Army; of the Puma and H225M helicopters, as well as A400M and C130, for the Air Force; and of the

---

29 "Race for Hypersonic Weapons Heats Up as France Joins 'Stealth by Speed' Contest," 2019.

30 Conversation with senior French defense official D, April 2019; Sénat, 2018c; Florence Parly, speech at the 53rd Paris Air Show, June 20, 2019b.

31 Laurent Lagneau, "Les C-160 Gabriel Seront Remplacés par Trois Avions Falcon de Guerre Électronique," *Zone Militaire*, March 1, 2018a; Parly, 2019b.

32 Michel Cabirol, "Disponibilité des Aéronefs Militaires: C'est Vraiment Très, Très Alarmant!" *La Tribune*, February 20, 2018a. "Availability rate" is our translation for the French "disponibilité technique," which is defined as a system's "ability to accomplish safely one of the functions for which it was conceived, in under six hours, given the support system in place" (translation from Sénat, 2017b, p. 9, fn. 1).

33 Sénat, 2018c.

34 French Defense Minister Florence Parly quoted in Anne Bauer, "Disponibilité des Avions de Combat: Parly Tape du Poing sur la Table," *Les Echos*, December 11, 2017.

NH90 helicopters and the maritime patrol aircraft Atlantique 2 for the Navy.[35] Although assets deployed on theaters of operation were, overall, at an 80-percent readiness level, those that were not deployed were at a 30-percent readiness level, creating challenges for French forces' ability to train and exercise.[36] Overall, the 2017 report found that the level of readiness of aircraft was insufficient for the French Air Force to fulfill even the low end of its operational contracts, which are the different types of contingencies that the French Air Force should be able to respond to concurrently, as set out in the LPM).[37] A report to the Sénat in July 2018 further underscored the severity of the situation for military helicopters, with only 171 available out of a total of 467 (36 percent), but assessed that this compromised only the high end of the Air Force's operational contracts.[38] In a hearing before the Sénat in October 2018, Air Force Chief of Staff General Philippe Lavigne also stated that some fleets—the A400Ms, Mirage 2000Ds, C-130s, and Pumas—were "objectively too weak" in terms of availability for training and operations.[39]

Several factors explain this readiness issue. French systems have had to perform in demanding operational environments—the Sahel, the Middle East—where heat and sand damage aircraft and helicopters.[40] Second, although the budget devoted to maintenance increased by 25 percent from 2012 to 2016, maintenance costs soared for some systems—an 81-percent increase, for instance, for the Caracal.[41] Yet the situation cannot be entirely blamed on operational demands, as Parly underlined in December 2017 that lack of readiness of French

---

35 Cabirol, 2018a.

36 Cabirol, 2018a.

37 Cabirol, 2018a.

38 Sénat, *Rapport d'Information Fait au Nom de la Commission des Finances (1) Sur la Disponibilité des Hélicoptères du Ministère des Armées*, Paris, July 11, 2018a, pp. 14–16.

39 Sénat, 2018e.

40 Lamigeon, 2017.

41 Christian Menanteau and Loic Farge, "Armée: Florence Parly S'Attaque aux Défaillances de la Maintenance des Avions," *RTL Radio*, December 12, 2017.

air assets has been an issue for 15 years.[42] Design and allocation of maintenance contracts represent a third, and key, problem. Tigre helicopters, for instance, are maintained through 37 different contracts, leading to a dilution of responsibilities and reduced effectiveness.[43] In December 2017, Parly announced the creation of a new Aeronautical Maintenance Directorate, whose first measures included extending the duration of maintenance contracts; reducing the number of different contractors for a given system; and introducing a performance clause in contracts.[44] Priority for the implementation of these changes was given to those systems with the lowest readiness, such as Atlantique 2 patrol aircraft, A400M transport aircraft, and helicopters.[45]

Some Challenges Remain

In addition to the unsatisfactory readiness of aircraft, which France is currently addressing, other challenges include rebuilding and training a strong Air Force after years of budget cuts, improving suppression of enemy air defenses (SEAD) capabilities, and increasing small stockpiles of munitions.

The Air Force was the service most affected by the downsizing of military personnel that took place under the previous LPM (2014–2019), leading to issues of recruitment and retention.[46] Lavigne noted that the high tempo of operations in Africa prevented more-experienced pilots from being able to train younger ones, and pilots who were heavily involved in operations in Africa need to re-train for full-spectrum

---

42 Bauer, 2017.

43 Bauer, 2017.

44 Pierre Tran, "France Creates Office to Improve Military Aircraft Readiness," *Defense News*, December 12, 2017b; Michel Cabirol, "Comment le Ministère des Armées Veut Améliorer la Disponibilité des Avions et des Hélicoptères," *La Tribune*, August 23, 2018b; Léo Barnier, "Quatre Questions à Monique Legrand-Larroche, Directrice de la DMAé," *Le Journal de l'Aviation*, May 24, 2018.

45 Barnier, 2018; Cabirol, 2018b.

46 Sénat, 2018e.

operations.[47] As a result, efforts are being made to improve operational readiness of Air Force personnel, with an increase of flying hours from 164 hours per year per fighter pilot in 2018 to 180 hours in 2023.[48] France is also investing in a new generation of trainer aircraft, the Pilatus PC21, which simulates flight on a Rafale and became operational in early 2019.[49] It is also worth noting that the modernization of capabilities (e.g., FCAS, upgraded radars) required for nuclear missions has a spillover effect on conventional missions.[50] Even when France was most involved in operations in Africa, the necessity to maintain proficiency for the air component of the nuclear deterrence means that pilots were still trained for full-spectrum operations and continued to practice high-end missions.[51]

Yet France's ambitions to conduct all types of missions are constrained by its limited SEAD capabilities[52] and by a lack of training for pilots in nonpermissive or semipermissive environments,[53] although the April 2018 French air strikes against chemical weapons storage sites in Syria (Operation Hamilton) did represent an opportunity for France to test its ability to perform precision strikes in a coalition.[54] Lavigne called for France to maintain its "participation [in] large exercises" to train with other forces for coalition operations, particularly

---

47 Sénat, 2018e.

48 Sénat, 2018e.

49 Parly, 2019b.

50 Sénat, 2018e.

51 Conversation with senior French defense official B, March 2019.

52 Jean-Christophe Noël, Morgan Paglia, and Elie Tenenbaum, *Les Armées Françaises Face aux Menaces Anti-Aériennes de Nouvelle Génération*, Paris: French Institute of International Relations, No. 86, December 2018, p. 29.

53 Noël, Paglia, and Tenenbaum, 2018, pp. 32–33.

54 France launched 12 missiles, but one of the five Rafales in the operation could not launch a SCALP missile, a failure attributed to missile malfunction (Fourt, 2018; Philippe Martinat, "Syrie: Des Ratés Dans l'Opération Hamilton," *Le Parisien*, April 20, 2018; Laurent Lagneau, "Syrie: La Marine Nationale a Tiré les Enseignements des Ratés de l'Opération Hamilton," *Zone Militaire*, November 30, 2018e; Charlie Gao, "Why France's Own 'Tomahawk' Missile Is in Serious Trouble," *National Interest*, November 19, 2018).

for air missions into semipermissive or nonpermissive environments.[55] He noted that the French response to the anti-access/area denial (A2/AD) challenge includes the Rafale, the FCAS, the FC/ASW, new active radars, and CUGE[56] and that he expects to "get back by the end of 2018 to a level that allows [the Air Force] to undertake crisis management operations."[57]

Finally, the Air Force—like other French services—has limited munition stocks, which makes some missions particularly challenging. Destruction of enemy air defense missions, for instance, which would allow a French raid to penetrate defended territory by destroying its air defenses, would require the use of large numbers of SCALP-EG missiles or naval cruise missiles that are not currently in stock—although this situation will improve when the *Suffren*-class submarines receive their planned 200 naval cruise missiles.[58] General purpose bombs are still available in insufficient numbers, and new orders are only expected at the end of the LPM.[59]

---

[55] Sénat, 2018e.

[56] Sénat, 2018e; the FCAS and FC/ASW, however, are long-term projects and will not be available for quite some time.

[57] Sénat, 2018e.

[58] Noël, Paglia, and Tenenbaum, 2018, pp. 30–31.

[59] Sénat, 2018e. One anecdote illustrates France's shortage of munitions. During the opening days of the French intervention in Mali in 2013, the French Air Force at the last minute had to change a planned bombing run in which the Rafales involved were supposed to fire A2SM missiles. Because the logistical chain could not provide the needed missiles in time, the Rafale had to carry guided gravity bombs instead. These yielded satisfactory results, but recourse to the bombs rather than the missiles meant that aircraft had to stay over the targets longer at a time when the French suspected the adversary possessed ground-to-air missiles (Notin, 2014, p. 212).

CHAPTER FIVE

Navy Capabilities

The French Navy component of the nuclear deterrent mission has helped stem the erosion of high-end conventional capabilities[1]—as it has for the French Air Force—and is largely driving the Navy's modernization process. France's FREMMs, for instance, are designed to cover all contingencies, including escorting ballistic missile submarines (SSBNs).[2] Some key priorities of the Navy include maintaining open sea lines of communication, particularly for its submarines; modernizing the fleet; maintaining power projection capabilities; and increasing stocks of munitions and munitions-related training.

The Navy, like its sister services, is roughly half the size it was at the end of the Cold War. In the Cold War it counted about 75,000 personnel, with under 30 percent consisting of conscripts.[3] Today, the number stands at about 35,000.[4] In 1985, the Navy had a fleet of 147 combat and support vessels;[5] the number now stands at 88, according to Janes.[6]

---

1 Conversation with French researchers on defense issues, March 2019.

2 Conversation with French researchers on defense issues, March 2019.

3 Chaumont, 1980, pp. 42, 76.

4 Ministère des Armées, Actualités, *Les Chiffres Clés de la Défense 2018,* Paris, 2018.

5 See the second annex to Patrick Boureille, "L'Outil Naval Français et la Sortie de la Guerre Froide (1985–1994)," *Revue Historique des Armées*, No. 245, December 15, 2006.

6 Janes, "France—Navy," March 10, 2020.

Maintaining Lines of Communication and Freedom of Navigation

Because SSBNs represent the key element of French naval dissuasion, France has made antisubmarine warfare a priority,[7] and Navy Chief of Staff Admiral Christophe Prazuck described antisubmarine warfare as an "absolutely fundamental challenge."[8] France's antisubmarine effort is largely carried out by the Atlantique 2 long-range maritime patrol aircraft. However, France has only 22 Atlantique 2 aircraft.[9] This makes them a scarce asset for the Navy, especially as these aircraft often play overland roles as well, such as in the Sahel, and a few are assigned to homeland defense. During Operation Serval, according to one study, there were six Atlantiques operating out of Dakar, representing nearly a third of the Navy's fleet and two-thirds of its operational crews.[10] As these aircraft have been in operation since the 1990s and present readiness issues, the LPM aims to renovate the existing fleet, which is deemed critical for the protection of French naval dissuasion.[11] France expects to receive two renovated Atlantique 2 aircraft in 2019, out of a total of 18 planned for modernization.[12]

In addition, France is co-developing with the United Kingdom a drone-based mine detection system called the Maritime Mine Countermeasures program,[13] which is the first step of a Future Mine Countermeasures Capability.[14] These drones are expected to be operational by

---

[7] Conversation with former senior French defense official A, March 2019.

[8] Sénat, 2018b.

[9] Laurent Lagneau, "Le Ministère des Armées Commande 6 Avions de Patrouille Maritime Atlantique 2 Modernisés," *Zone Militaire*, October 24, 2018c.

[10] Notin, 2014, p. 255.

[11] Conversation with former senior French defense official A, March 2019.

[12] Sénat, 2018b; Lagneau, 2018c.

[13] Sénat, 2018b. See also Richard Scott, "Euronaval 2018: Integration Activity Ramps Up for French/UK MMCM Programme," *Janes Navy International*, October 23, 2018.

[14] Ministère des Armées, Direction Générale de l'Armement, "Le Système de Lutte Anti-Mines Marines Future (SLAMF)," March 24, 2016.

2022,[15] but the program appears to be experiencing delays.[16] The Navy is also developing a tactical drone capability (the Système de Drone Aérien pour la Marine), which is expected to be operational in 2025.[17]

Renewing the Fleet and Improving Its Readiness

The French Navy is pursuing the modernization of the maritime nuclear deterrent and other assets. It will receive the first four (out of six) *Barracuda*-class nuclear attack submarines in 2019–2025 to replace the *Rubis* class.[18] These submarines will be equipped with Artemis heavy torpedoes, Exocet antiship missiles, and naval cruise missiles.[19] As for SSBNs, a third generation (succeeding the *Redoutable* and *Triomphant* classes) is expected in the 2030s.[20] France will equip its SSBNs with a new version of the M51 ballistic missile.[21]

The delivery of France's sixth FREMM is expected in 2019,[22] with the last three available by 2025.[23] As for tactical airborne early warning aircraft, France is planning to replace its E-2C Hawkeye with three of the E-2D Advanced version by 2025–2026. This aircraft features an improved radar and more autonomy.[24] Another ongoing project is the French-Italian FLOTLOG (Flotte Logistque) program, through which

---

15 Sénat, 2017b, p. 31.

16 Sénat, 2018b.

17 Sénat, 2017b, p. 30.

18 Nicholas Fiorenza, "Programmed for the Future: France Country Briefing," *Janes Defence Weekly*, July 18, 2018; Defense Industry Daily, "France's Future SSNs: The Barracuda Class," May 10, 2018.

19 Sénat, 2018d; Fiorenza, 2018.

20 "La Coûteuse Modernisation de la Dissuasion Nucléaire," 2018.

21 "La Coûteuse Modernisation de la Dissuasion Nucléaire," 2018.

22 Sénat, 2018b.

23 Fiorenza, 2018; Pierre Tran, "France Takes Delivery of Its 5th FREMM," *Defense News*, July 25, 2018a.

24 "FANAL 19: 30 Rafale M," *Le Fauteuil de Colbert*, February 12, 2019; Janes, "France—Navy," March 13, 2019.

the two countries codevelop logistical support ships. France plans to order three such ships in 2019 to have them in service between 2022 and 2027. A fourth ship might be added, which would be operational in 2029.[25] Table 5.1 provides a list of main items that will be added to France's naval arsenal in 2019–2025 and its ambitions for 2030.

Another Navy priority is improving availability of helicopters. Rather than maintaining its aging fleet of Alouette III and Lynx, France chose to rent H160s until the entire fleet can be replaced with NH 90s and Hélicoptères Interarmées Légers by 2030—a stop-gap solution deemed equivalent in cost but that allows for training on new equipment.[26]

Maintaining France's Power Projection Capabilities

With a nuclear-powered aircraft carrier—the *Charles de Gaulle*—and three *Mistral*-class amphibious assault ships, France is one of West-

Table 5.1
Expected Increase in Number of Selected Main Systems by 2025 (Navy)

System	Number as of 2019	Expected Number in 2025	Ambition in 2030
Barracuda	0	4	6
FREMM air defense	0	2	2
FREMM antisubmarine warfare	5	6	6
Retrofitted Atlantique 2	0	18	18
FTI (frigates of intermediate size)	0	2	5
NH 90 NFH (NATO frigate helicopter)	22	27	27

SOURCE: Adapted from de Legge, 2018a, p. 59.

[25] Vincent Groizeleau, "FLOTLOG: L'Accord Franco-Italien Signé," *Mer et Marine*, October 25, 2018.

[26] Sénat, 2018b.

ern Europe's most capable nations with respect to power projection. In 2017–2018, the *Charles de Gaulle* was off line for a major midlife maintenance operation that modernized its combat system, information systems, communications, and radars.[27] Its first mission after this overhaul took place in Syria, in support of the international coalition against the Islamic State.[28] The *Charles de Gaulle* also plays an important role in France's defense diplomacy. The ship is supposed to conduct joint exercises with the Egyptian and Indian Navies, and the Navy has reinforced its partnership with its counterparts in India and Japan.[29] Finally, it enables French forces to develop interoperability with allies, and the *Charles de Gaulle* carrier group has incorporated ships from Portugal, Denmark, Italy, and the United Kingdom.[30]

The *Charles de Gaulle* has been operational since 2001 and should remain so for about another 25 years; studies for its replacement have already begun.[31] The specifics of the next French aircraft carrier are still largely unknown, including whether France will choose a nuclear reactor for propulsion or switch to gas turbines and diesel generators, as the United Kingdom decided to do with its new *Queen Elizabeth* class of aircraft carriers.[32] France also has to decide whether to continue with the system of steam catapults currently in use or to switch to the electromagnetic aircraft launch system that now equips USS *Gerald R. Ford*–class aircraft carriers;[33] France appears keen to maintain the

---

[27] The *Charles de Gaulle* is immobilized, on average, every five years for maintenance (Fourt, 2018).

[28] Jean-François Rosnoblet, "Le *Charles de Gaulle*, un Porte-Avions Taillé pour la Guerre et la Diplomatie," Reuters, March 8, 2019.

[29] Rosnoblet, 2019; conversation with senior French defense officials, March 2019.

[30] Rosnoblet, 2019.

[31] Fourt, 2018.

[32] Laurent Lagneau, "La Construction du Prochain Porte-Avions de la Marine Nationale Sera Pleine de Défis," *Zone Militaire*, November 7, 2017c.

[33] Lagneau, 2017c.

larger range gained through catapults and to avoid the additional weight brought on by the electromagnetic aircraft launch system.[34]

Another unresolved question is whether the replacement for the *Charles de Gaulle* should have a sister ship. This would make it possible to continue operations with one aircraft carrier while the other one undergoes maintenance. The French leadership has expressed its preference for having two aircraft carriers instead of one on several occasions since 1980, but budgetary constraints have always prevented this from happening.[35] The LPM funds studies for the design of the *Charles de Gaulle*'s successor, assuaging some concerns that France might get rid of its aircraft carrier program altogether; Parly suggested that the question of whether there should be one such successor carrier or two remains open.[36]

A Need for Increased Training, Including on Munitions

Navy personnel are trained for high-intensity conflict, including antisurface warfare, antisubmarine warfare, and antiaerial warfare.[37] Training time for Navy personnel was reduced by 20 percent over the past ten years,[38] but it is on the increase again, with an objective to get to 110 days at sea per blue water Navy vessel.[39] While the French aircraft carrier was out of commission during its mid-life overhaul, 350 Navy aviators and support personnel were given the opportunity to train in April–May 2018 onboard the *George H. W. Bush* aircraft carrier out of Norfolk, Virginia, so that they could be immediately operational when

---

34 Conversation with senior French defense officials, March 2019.

35 Laurent Lagneau, "La Question de Doter la Marine Nationale d'un ou de Deux Porte-Avions 'Reste Ouverte' Selon Mme Parly," *Zone Militaire*, September 10, 2018b.

36 Lagneau, 2018b.

37 Conversation with former senior French defense official A, March 2019.

38 Sénat, 2018b.

39 Sénat, 2018c.

the *Charles de Gaulle* was released from the docks.[40] This training was also an opportunity for working on interoperability more generally.[41]

The Navy's ability to train on complex munitions appears more limited, largely because of limited stocks.[42] During Operation Hamilton on April 14, 2018, two FREMMs could not launch their new naval cruise missiles and had to rely on the reserve FREMM that was escorting them.[43] The malfunction was attributed to computer issues on the FREMM.[44] French Parliamentarian Jacques Maroussian described some of the lessons learned by the Navy following this operation, including the need for strengthening operational readiness, a need for "much higher training level for target practice, particularly for complex munitions" and the need to "rethink the tactical use of our weapons" in an environment where increasingly sophisticated A2/AD prevails.[45] French Navy Chief Admiral Christophe Prazuck highlighted that some investments were being made to replenish stocks of munitions that are "low" to make sure that "every ship and aircraft crew can shoot at least one complex munition [missile or torpedo] every other year."[46]

---

40 Mark D. Faram, "French Aircrews Ready to Train in Norfolk," *Navy Times*, March 27, 2018.

41 Faram, 2018.

42 Sénat, 2018b.

43 Fourt, 2018; Martinat, 2018; Lagneau, 2018e.

44 Gao, 2018. Operation Hamilton was the first time these new naval cruise missiles were launched in an operation (Assemblée Nationale, "Avis Fait au Nom de la Commission de la Defense Nationale et des Forces Armées sur le Projet de Loi de Finances pour 2019 (No. 1255), Tome V, Défense, Préparation et Emploi des Forces: Marine," October 12, 2018).

45 Translation from Gao, 2018.

46 Translation from Sénat, 2018b.

CHAPTER SIX

Space, Cyber, and Intelligence Capabilities

The LPM plans for major investments in the space and cyber domains. Space is perceived as a critical enabler for "high on the spectrum" capabilities because of the role played by military and commercial satellites in ensuring safe communications during operations, particularly for such networked capabilities as SCORPION.[1] Similarly, the need to defeat cyberattacks that could cripple France's ability to carry out nuclear or conventional missions and threaten its critical infrastructure has prompted French decisionmakers to devote more resources to enhancing cyber capabilities.

Space

The LPM commits 3.6 billion euros to space capabilities and their modernization; in late July 2019, it was announced that an additional 700 million euros would be devoted to this domain until 2025.[2] France's interest in this area is not new, as investments in space capabilities had already doubled in value between 2008 and 2014.[3] The 2017 Strategic Review describes outer space as "a domain of strategic

1 Conversation with French researchers on defense issues, March 2019.

2 Sénat, 2018d; Murielle Delaporte, "From Paris to Orbit: France's New Space Strategy," *Breaking Defense*, January 3, 2019; Ministère des Armées, Actualités, "Florence Parly Dévoile la Stratégie Spatiale Française de Défense," January 9, 2020.

3 Delaporte, 2019.

and military rivalry,"[4] and Parly released a French Space Defense Strategy in July 2019.[5]

French officials have cited various security concerns related to space. In September 2018, Parly revealed that a Russian satellite had been caught spying on the French-Italian satellite Athena-Fidus, which is used for military communications.[6] On that occasion, she mentioned concern over the increasing capabilities of state actors in the domain of antisatellite weapons and made clear that France intended to be ready to protect its interests in space against such threats.[7] Parly also cited the need for better management of traffic in space.[8] An increasingly large presence of debris threatens space safety and risks damaging satellites that are critical for military and civilian uses.[9]

Cooperation with the United States is strong in this domain and provides an additional motivation for France to remain at a high level of technology so that such cooperation continues.[10] Accordingly, France is engaged in an extensive modernization program of its military and commercial satellites, often in cooperation with European and international partners. In December 2018, France launched the first of its Composante Spatiale Optique (Optical Space Component, or CSO) military reconnaissance satellite, with three more planned in 2020, to replace the Helios satellite system.[11] The CSO system was developed by France in cooperation with Germany, Sweden, and Belgium and will

---

[4] République Française, 2017a, p. 45, paragraph 129.

[5] Pierre Alonso, "L'Armée Française Se Prépare à La Guerre des Étoiles," *Libération*, July 25, 2019.

[6] Florence Parly, "Statement on Space Defense," speech in Toulouse, France, September 7, 2018. See also John Leicester and Sylvie Corbet, "France Says Russia Satellite Spied in 'Star Wars' Hostility," Associated Press, September 7, 2018; and John Irish, "France Accuses Russia of Spying on Military from Space," Reuters, September 7, 2018.

[7] Leicester and Corbet, 2018.

[8] Parly, 2018.

[9] Conversation with senior French defense official B, March 2019; République Française, 2017a, p. 45, paragraph 132.

[10] Conversation with senior French defense official B, March 2019.

[11] Delaporte, 2019.

provide data to the Multinational Space-Based Imaging System, a program that allows France, Belgium, Germany, Greece, Italy, and Spain to share space-based intelligence.[12] CSO's successor, the IRIS program, was announced by Parly at the 2019 Paris Air Show. France also plans to launch two more communication satellites during 2020–2022 and is in a partnership with Australia to develop satellite technologies with advanced sensor capacities.[13]

France's new space strategy calls for continued cooperation with the United States, described as an "essential ally for [French] military spatial operations." Europe is mentioned in the strategy as an actor that should have "its own capacities" allowing it to be a "credible partner" for the United States. Yet the strategy is also very clear that, with regard to military spatial capabilities, pooling will be limited, as "nations keep sovereign control over their capabilities."[14]

Cyber and Intelligence

Cyber and intelligence have been described as being among of the "winners" of the LPM, for 330 of the 450 new positions created within the Ministry of Defense in 2019 fall into these two categories, with more new positions coming up between 2019 and 2022.[15] The LPM commits 1.6 billion euros for cyber alone.[16] The budgets of the three intelligence agencies under the authority of the Defense Ministry—the Direction du Renseignement et de la Sécurité de la Défense, the Direc-

---

12 Delaporte, 2019; Centre National d'Études Spatiales, "CSO/MUSIS," April 9, 2018.

13 Delaporte, 2019; Ministère de l'Europe et des Affaires Étrangères, "Australia, France Join to Build Space Industry Capability," September 18, 2018.

14 Ministère des Armées, *Stratégie Spatiale de Défense*, Paris, 2019, p. 38.

15 Vincent Lamigeon, "Budget des Armées 2019: Qui Sont les Gagnants?" *Challenges*, September 27, 2018; Sénat, 2018c.

16 Philippe Chapleau, "Cyberdéfense. L'Armée Passe à l'Offensive," *Ouest-France*, January 18, 2019.

tion du Renseignement Militaire, and the Direction Générale de la Sécurité Extérieure—are planned to increase by 15 percent in 2019.[17]

The focus on cyber is not recent, and the 2013 White Paper on Defense and National Security had already described this domain as a national priority for the French military.[18] The 2017 Strategic Review reiterated this position[19] and made clear that

> [i]n cyberspace, certain attacks might be regarded as armed aggression, due to their scale and severity. A major cyberattack may, given the damage it could cause, justify invoking legitimate defense under Article 51 of the UN Charter.[20]

In a January 2019 statement, Parly underscored the severity of the threat, with 700 security incidents against the Defense Ministry's networks in 2017 and more in 2018.[21] She also noted that the attack that targeted the French Navy in late 2017 had been attributed by some sources to Turla, a group responsible for failed and successful past attempts against, among others, Finnish, Swiss, and German ministries; Estonia claims that Turla is associated with Russia's intelligence services.[22]

France has undertaken organizational changes and new doctrines. In January 2017, France created a cyber operational command tasked specifically with defending military networks, as well as those

---

17 Sénat, 2018d.

18 Ministère des Armées, "La Cyberdéfense," October 17, 2018b.

19 It notes, for instance, that "The capacity to take action in cyberspace and in the informational domain is becoming increasingly accessible. As a result, our societies, populations, government services and businesses are more directly exposed to interference or malicious actions that may have major consequences" (République Française, *Strategic Review of Defence and National Security 2017—Key Points*, 2017b).

20 République Française, 2017a, p. 33, paragraph 90.

21 Chapleau 2019; Gabriel Thierry, "Ces Opérations Venues du Froid Qui Inquiètent Florence Parly," *L'Essor*, January 21, 2019. See also Jean-Dominique Merchet, "Florence Parly Révèle une Cyberattaque Très Sérieuse Contre les Armées," *Secret Défense*, January 18, 2019.

22 Council on Foreign Relations, "Turla," undated.

of critical infrastructures.[23] In February 2018, the Secretariat-General for Defense and National Security, a cross-governmental agency placed under the authority of the Prime Minister's office, released a cyberdefense strategic review.[24] In January 2019, France also partially released its first cyber offense doctrine, which includes a section on international cooperation.[25]

---

23 François Delerue, Alix Desforges, and Aude Géry, "A Close Look at France's New Military Cyber Strategy," *War on the Rocks*, April 23, 2019.

24 Secrétariat Général de la Défense et la Sécurité Nationale, *Revue Stratégique de Cyberdéfense*, Paris, February 12, 2018.

25 Chapleau, 2019.

CHAPTER SEVEN

Political and Societal Constraints to Use of Force

Although an assessment of military capabilities provides a fairly good perspective on whether a given country could respond to a range of contingencies, it says nothing of whether political leaders would be willing to use force to respond to such contingencies. Political, legal, and societal factors play an important role in constraining the use of force. In this chapter, we examine how these factors play out in France in general and against Russia in particular. Our final section examines existing commitments of French forces that might limit French decisionmakers' ability to reassign forces to respond to a contingency in Eastern Europe.

Constraints to Using Force

There are few political constraints to the use of French forces. Since de Gaulle established foreign and security policy as the domaine réservé of the chief of the executive branch, the decision to engage armed forces abroad has largely remained a prerogative of the president, regardless of his political orientation.[1] Although President Nicolas Sarkozy (2007–2012) made an effort to limit this power by requiring parliamentary approval of military deployments past the first four months

---

[1] Jolyon Howorth, "François Mitterrand and the 'Domaine Réservé': From Cohabitation to the Gulf War," *French Politics and Society*, Vol. 10, No. 1, Winter 1992.

of engagement,[2] the president's ability to commit forces remains fairly large. In the past, even unpopular presidents have found support for military interventions. For instance, in December 2013, President François Hollande received favorable opinions from only 37 percent of French surveyed, but Operation Serval was supported by 75 percent of the population.[3] Support has historically been strong for French military interventions more broadly. In 2017, an Ifop poll for the French ministry of armed forces found that 59 percent of respondents supported Operation Barkhane; 77 percent supported Operation Sentinelle; and 85 percent supported Operation Chammal in Syria and Iraq.[4] Furthermore, the French public is highly supportive of its military. In a January 2019 poll on institutions that the French trust most, 74 percent of respondents declared having "a lot of trust" or "some trust" in the military, making it the third most-trusted institution according to the poll.[5]

Constraints to Using Force Against Russia

Since he became president in May 2017, Macron followed Hollande's "firmness and dialogue" approach to Russia.[6] Having been personally targeted by an aggressive disinformation campaign shortly before the 2017 presidential election,[7] Macron has been particularly vocal

---

[2] Estelle Shirbon, "France's Sarkozy Secures Constitutional Reform," Reuters, July 21, 2008.

[3] Ifop, *Les Indices de Popularité*, January 2013, p. 7; "Sondage: 75% des Français Soutiennent l'Intervention au Mali," *Le Parisien*, January 15, 2013.

[4] Eliot Granveau, "Sondage. Les Français Soutiennent Nos Opérations Extérieures," *Ouest-France*, April 21, 2017; Laurent Lagneau, "Fort Soutien de l'Opinion Publique aux Opérations Menées par les Armées Françaises," *Zone Militaire*, April 21, 2017a.

[5] The French police received a score identical to the armed forces. By comparison, the equivalent percentages were 13 percent and 9 percent for social media and political parties, respectively, which were at the bottom of the ranking. (OpinionWay for Cevipof/SciencesPo, "En Qu(o)i les Français Ont-Ils Confiance Aujourd'hui?" January 2019, p. 34).

[6] Conversation with senior French defense officials, March 2019.

[7] "French Presidential Candidate Macron Target of Russian 'Fake News,' His Party Chief Claims," *DeutscheWelle*, February 13, 2017; Adam Nossiter, David E. Sanger, and Nicole Perlroth, "Hackers Came, but the French Were Prepared," *New York Times*, May 9, 2017.

against potential Russian attempts at influencing French politics, calling Russia Today and Sputnik "organs of influence, of propaganda" in front of President Vladimir Putin during their June 2017 meeting.[8] Yet Macron's approach is also a pragmatic one, and he has repeatedly called for re-engaging with Russia. In June 2018, he called for a "restart" of the "dynamic" with Putin (while supporting Russia's exclusion from the G7 Summit planned to take place in southern France in August 2019).[9] In August 2018, he suggested that the government should "rethink our relation with Russia,"[10] calling for more cooperation and noting that "on matters like cybersecurity, defense, strategic relationships, we could envisage the outlines of a new relationship between Russia and the EU" to increase stability in Europe.[11] On September 9, 2019, the French and Russian ministers of defense and ministers of foreign affairs met in Moscow, resuming an annual bilateral meeting that had been suspended in 2014, after Russia's invasion of Crimea.[12]

Macron will likely be running for re-election in 2022, barring any catastrophic event or a popularity so low that he would choose, like Hollande, not to run. It is worth noting that out of the four candidates who scored highest in the first round of the 2017 presidential election, three supported moderately or strongly pro-Russian positions, such as the removal of sanctions, with Macron the only one to advocate a hard line on this issue. Although the two-round electoral system makes it unlikely that the extreme-right or extreme-left wins the presidency in

---

8 James McAuley, "French President Macron Blasts Russian State-Owned Media as 'Propaganda,'" *Washington Post*, May 29, 2017.

9 Marine Pennetier, "Macron Souhaite 'Réenclencher Une Dynamique' avec Poutine Avant le G7," Reuters, June 11, 2019.

10 Emmanuel Macron, "Déclaration de M. Emmanuel Macron, Président de la République, sur la Défense Européenne à Helsinki le 30 Août 2018," speech in Helsinki, August 30, 2018.

11 Macron quoted in Anne Kauranen, "It's Time for Realism in EU-Russia Ties: France's Macron," Reuters, August 30, 2018; he also noted that such increased cooperation would be conditional on progress on different fronts, including the conflict in Ukraine.

12 Gregory Viscusi, "French Ministers Visit Moscow in First Such Meeting Since 2014," *Bloomberg*, September 8, 2019; Marc Semo, "Macron Assume Son Virage Russe," *Le Monde*, September 7, 2019.

2022, even the victory of a more mainstream party, such as the conservative Les Républicains, might result in a more accommodating policy toward Russia.

Yet Russia is not particularly popular among the French: According to a 2018 Pew Research Center poll, 66 percent of the French have a negative view of Russia, while 30 percent have a positive view.[13] An earlier poll from the same organization indicated that in 2017, 53 percent of French respondents declared that their country "should use military force to defend a NATO ally if it got into a serious military conflict with Russia," up from 47 percent in 2015. This figure puts France higher than Spain, the United Kingdom, or Germany in terms of public support to use its military to defend an ally against Russia.[14]

Constraints to Deploying Forces

A more important constraint to France deploying sizable troops in Eastern Europe relates to France's ability—or lack thereof—to move troops that are currently used for other operations. France's demanding operational commitments mean that staging and sustaining anything larger than a brigade-sized force would require it to strip troops from other activities. Given the importance Paris gives to its Sahel operations and the political sensitivity of downsizing Operation Sentinelle too drastically, French decisionmakers might be reluctant to follow that path. This constraint is likely to be a lasting one, as there is no clear exit strategy for either Operation Barkhane or Operation Sentinelle.

In addition to foreign and domestic military interventions, French forces are also "pinned" by other, more-routine tasks that are of high value for France. For instance, an important mission of the French Navy is law enforcement at sea (Action de l'État en Mer), which protects France's interests over its extensive maritime domain—the second-

---

13 Pew Research Center, "Image of Putin, Russia Suffers Internationally," December 6, 2018.

14 Bruce Stokes, "NATO's Image Improves on Both Sides of the Atlantic: European Faith in American Military Support Largely Unchanged," Pew Research Center, May 23, 2017, p. 15.

largest after that of the United States—and includes such missions as securing maritime security and safety, controlling fisheries, combating drug trafficking and unregulated migration, and preventing sea pollution.[15] Some of France's Navy assets could not be reassigned without opening vulnerabilities on this front.[16] The French Navy also performs a variety of other duties that France would be reluctant to abandon. Two examples are support to operations against the Islamic State (Operation Chammal) and the recent deployment of a carrier task force (Mission Foch) to the eastern Mediterranean associated both with Operation Chammal and diplomatic tensions related to Libya and natural gas exploitation.[17] In addition, approximately 1,000 personnel and several fighter squadrons maintain France's air safety permanent posture (Posture Permanente de Sûreté Aérienne) that monitors (and potentially intercepts) threats in the national airspace.[18] Some key air assets that are dedicated to the nuclear deterrent mission—such as fighters or air refueling assets—could also be used for a large-scale conventional conflict, but there might be some reluctance to reassigning them. Overall, this puts limits on the volume of capabilities that France might be willing to shift toward a contingency in Eastern Europe.

---

15 Government of France, "Secrétariat Général de la Mer (SGMER)—Action de l'État en Mer," undated.

16 Conversation with former senior French defense official A, March 2019.

17 Xavier Vavasseur, "French Carrier Strike Group Begins 'Foch' Deployment," *USNI News*, January 23, 2020.

18 Ministère des Armées, Actualités, "[Focus] La Posture Permanente de Sûreté Aérienne," February 20, 2016; conversation with French researchers on defense issues, March 2019.

CHAPTER EIGHT

Conclusions and Implications for U.S. Policy

Could France support a U.S.-led war effort in Eastern Europe now or in the next ten years? The answer is yes: France has maintained full-spectrum capabilities and training; it is devoting renewed spending to defense for ambitious modernization objectives, including at the high end of the spectrum (for instance, the FCAS and hypersonic weapons); and there is strong political and public support for military interventions and support to France's allies. In addition, France's operations in Mali, in Central African Republic, and against low-tech adversaries (i.e., jihadist groups and insurgents) have not resulted in a complete shift toward expeditionary warfare capabilities and skills. For example, even when engaged in low-intensity operations, French forces have deployed (and tested) equipment designed for higher-intensity operations, such as the CAESAR, digital networking technology, and the Rafale.[1] That said, the French commitment to such conflict zones as the Sahel means that France is not about to restructure its forces to tailor them exclusively for a high-end conflict. Having embraced the idea of a middle segment intended to be good enough for the highest and lowest ends of the conflict spectrum, France is unlikely to change the basic orientation of its armed forces for the foreseeable future.

There are limits to what France could do on a hypothetical eastern front: Its military has little depth overall and could not sustain a long campaign, and some of the capabilities it might need would likely not be reassigned. The French can manage a low-intensity conflict like

[1] Conversation with senior French defense officials, March 2019.

Operation Barkhane for an extended period of time, but their ability to sustain a high-intensity fight is less clear because of France's lack of both human capital and materials.[2] Overall, France's contribution to a large-scale conventional war in Eastern Europe would likely be forthcoming but limited in its sustainability.

There are capability areas with potential for increased U.S.-French collaboration that might improve France's ability to fight a conventional war in Eastern Europe. This conclusion highlights the capability areas that have been found by RAND research to be most critical in the event of a NATO response to Russian aggression in Europe. It then highlights which of these capabilities France might be best positioned to contribute or to further develop through U.S.-French collaboration.

Matching Operational Needs to Capabilities

From the end of the Cold War until Russia's invasions of Ukraine in 2014, force planners in the U.S. Department of Defense had regarded Europe and NATO as exporters of security; that is, a place where U.S. and allied forces could train for and prepare to undertake "out of area" missions in such places as Afghanistan, the Middle East, and Africa. Since 2014, U.S. force planning has focused on enhancing the NATO alliance's capabilities and posturing to deter and defeat aggression on NATO's eastern flank.

Wargaming and analysis reveal serious gaps in NATO's ability to blunt a large-scale Russian attack.[3] Given NATO's current posture, the allies could confront a situation in which their ground forces were badly outnumbered and outgunned by the force that Russia could deploy to the borders of the Baltic States within one to two weeks.

---

[2] Conversation with senior French defense official C, March 2019.

[3] Large-scale aggression is not the only threat facing NATO members. Russia has demonstrated both the capability and the intent to subvert domestic political affairs and social stability in countries along Russia's periphery and beyond. NATO members have responded to these sorts of challenges in a variety of ways, including stepped-up intelligence and information sharing, enhanced cyber monitoring and defense, combined training of special forces, and strengthened internal security programs.

NATO's air forces would find it difficult and time-consuming to suppress the network of surface-to-air missile systems that Russia would deploy in the region, limiting NATO ability to provide fire support to the ground defense. Air bases, command and control centers, logistics concentrations, lines of communication, air- and seaports of debarkation, and other rear-area assets could come under attack from Russian ballistic and cruise missiles. Military space constellations that provide reconnaissance; communications; and position, navigation, and timing services could be disrupted by cyber, electronic jamming, and kinetic attacks. In short, NATO nations concerned about the possibility of Russian threats to allies along NATO's eastern flank have ample reasons to be dissatisfied with the current situation.[4]

Since 2016, Supreme Headquarters Allied Powers Europe, U.S. European Command, and selected NATO member states have taken steps to address key shortfalls in NATO's deterrent posture.[5] However, more needs to be done before the allies can be confident in convincing an aggressive Russian leader that a low-cost coup de main attack is infeasible. Key areas that need to be addressed include the following:

- Forward deployed heavy ground forces. The multinational battalions in the Baltic States, combined with the U.S. armored brigade combat teams rotationally deployed in Europe, could act as the nucleus of a NATO force to confront invaders. Previous RAND research suggests that an additional brigade combat team

[4] In multiple iterations of a wargame assessing the military balance today, NATO forces were never able to prevent Russian forces from quickly overrunning important terrain in the Baltic States. Russian forces were able to reach one or more of the Baltic States' capital cities within 36–60 hours (David A. Shlapak and Michael W. Johnson, *Reinforcing Deterrence on NATO's Eastern Flank*, Santa Monica, Calif.: RAND Corporation, RR-1253-A, 2016).

[5] Key improvements include the deployment of three multinational NATO battalions and one U.S. battalion to the Baltic States and a U.S. armored brigade combat team on a rotational basis; prepositioning of equipment and ammunition for additional U.S. ground forces; improvements to infrastructure at U.S. bases, airfields, and training ranges and to transportation infrastructure in Central Europe; and expanded multinational exercises (Michelle Shevin-Coetzee, *The European Deterrence Initiative*, Washington, D.C.: Center for Strategic and Budgetary Assessments, 2019).

is needed at the outset of hostilities, followed by three more reinforcing brigade combat teams within a few days.[6]

- Self-propelled artillery, including rounds with area effects weapons.
- Improved means for providing ISR and targeting in contested environments. These could include distributed ground sensors, special operations forces, low-observable ("stealth") aircraft, and large numbers of small UAVs.
- Secure, anti-jam data links to connect sensors to control centers and control centers to shooters. Interoperability among allied forces will be essential.
- Large stocks of guided anti-armor weapons. Air-delivered weapons that can be launched from outside the range of Russian SAM systems will be particularly important.
- Improved weapons for SEAD, including electronic jamming systems. A new, fast-flying radar-homing missile should have a high priority. Low-cost, "stand-in" jamming systems might also be effective.
- Mobile short-range air defense systems for cruise missile defenses and for protecting maneuver forces from UAVs and attack helicopters. U.S. maneuver forces lack effective means for defeating attacks by fixed-wing aircraft, attack helicopters, and even slow-moving UAVs, and U.S. air bases can be damaged by large salvos of cruise missiles. Short-range air defense systems, such as the National Advanced Surface to Air Missile System, could provide an effective defensive layer.
- Enhancements to intratheater transportation assets and infrastructure. Mobility assets, such as heavy equipment transporters for armored vehicles, are in short supply in Central Europe. Logisticians are working to identify and eliminate transportation bottlenecks, such as bridges in critical areas that cannot support heavy forces.

---

6 Shlapak and Johnson, 2016.

Potential French Contributions

France's armed forces possess capabilities that could help meet some of the needs outlined above. These include heavy ground forces and artillery, as well as special operations forces. The French are practiced in joint operations, which surely will be a requirement in a conflict against Russia.[7] Capability areas that might benefit from increased U.S.-French collaboration include electronic warfare, countering of massed precision fires, the integration of airborne and terrestrial ISR systems, air defenses, and hardening of advanced technologies against threats—all capabilities that would be highly useful in countering a resurgent Russia. Aerial refueling aircraft and satellites for ISR and communications are also relevant capabilities. U.S. air forces might also benefit from the ability to operate in wartime from French air bases, particularly if those bases are protected from cruise missile attacks and well-stocked or readily resupplied with fuel.[8] France would likely welcome any program that allows it to develop its currently limited SEAD capabilities and ensures that, as one of our interlocutors put it, "a raid always goes through," which is an essential condition to credible deterrence and to successful interventions in a strategic environment where a number of France's adversaries use more and more-sophisticated air defense systems. In addition to capabilities that would help France reach these ambitions, cooperation programs to develop jam-resistant data links would be of particular value to France because networked warfare is becoming the new standard for its Army.

Although transatlantic relations have worsened, Macron has continued engagement with the United States, and the United States and France continue to enjoy a strong defense relationship through joint operations, personnel exchanges, multilateral exercises, intelligence

---

7 France's recent operations (Operations Serval, Barkhane, and Chammal) have all required extensive coordination between ground and air assets, with the latter including ground and carrier-based ISR and strike aircraft provided by the French Air Force and Navy. Operation Serval also involved the use of one of the French Navy's amphibious assault ships, the *Dixmude*.

8 U.S. aircraft also can operate off of France's aircraft carrier and its assault ships (and vice versa).

sharing, and other activities. France's 2017 Strategic Review describes the United States as a "fundamental partner, due to the convergence of their defense and security interests as well as a strong bilateral relation in the operational and intelligence domains."[9] France is also keen on developing interoperability (as evidenced by its concern that the future FCAS be interoperable with the F-35), as it recognizes that it will need partners for most missions, particularly high-end ones.[10] Although specific modes of cooperation would have to be devised for each capability in ways that preserve the interests of both U.S. and French defense industry firms involved, such cooperation could help France addresses its challenges in fighting high-end conventional wars more quickly.

---

9 République Française, 2017a, p. 58, paragraph 194.

10 Conversation with senior French defense official B, March 2019; conversation with French researchers on defense issues, March 2019.

References

Alonso, Pierre, "Méditerranée: Chaotique Cohabitation Entre Marines Russe et Française," *Libération*, September 20, 2018.

———, "L'Armée Française Se Prépare à La Guerre des Étoiles," *Libération*, July 25, 2019. As of April 20, 2020:
https://www.liberation.fr/france/2019/07/25/l-armee-francaise-se-prepare-a-la-guerre-des-etoiles_1742041

"AMX-10P Infantry Fighting Vehicle," *Military Today*, undated. As of May 1, 2020:
http://www.military-today.com/apc/amx_10p.htm

Armée de l'Air, "L'Armée de l'Air en Chiffres 2019–2020," April 21, 2020. As of July 17, 2020:
https://www.defense.gouv.fr/air/presentation/chiffres-cles/chiffres-cles-de-l-armee-de-l-air

Assemblée Nationale, "Avis Fait au Nom de la Commission de la Defense Nationale et des Forces Armées sur le Projet de Loi de Finances pour 2019 (No. 1255), Tome V, Défense, Préparation et Emploi des Forces: Marine," October 12, 2018. As of April 21, 2020:
http://www.assemblee-nationale.fr/15/budget/plf2019/a1306-tV.asp

Barnier, Léo, "Quatre Questions à Monique Legrand-Larroche, Directrice de la DMAé," *Le Journal de l'Aviation*, May 24, 2018.

Barrera, Bernard, *Opération Serval: Notes de Guerre*, Mali 2013. Paris : Éditions du Seuil, 2015,

Bauer, Anne, "Disponibilité des Avions de Combat: Parly Tape du Poing sur la Table," *Les Echos*, December 11, 2017.

Boureille, Patrick, "L'outil Naval Français et la Sortie de la Guerre Froide (1985–1994)," *Revue Historique des Armées*, No. 245, December 15, 2006, pp. 46–61.

Brunier, Camille, "[Bourget 2019] Le SCAF Se Dévoile, des Annonces Importantes dans l'Aéronautique et le Spatial Militaire," *Ministère des Armées*, June 18, 2019. As of April 21, 2020:
https://www.defense.gouv.fr/actualites/articles/bourget-2019-le-scaf-se-devoile-des-annonces-importantes-dans-l-aeronautique-et-le-spatial-militaire

Brustlein, Corentin, "Forces Nucléaires Francaises, Quel Renouvellement?" *Politique Étrangère*, Vol. 3, 2017, pp. 113–124.

Bunoust-Becques, Florian, "Du Sahel au Levant: Quelle Place pour l'Artillerie Française?" *Opérationnels—Soutien, Logistique, Défense, Sécurité*, January 8, 2019. As of April 21, 2020:
https://operationnels.com/2019/01/08/du-sahel-au-levant-quelle-place-pour-lartillerie-francaise

Cabirol, Michel, "Disponibilité des Aéronefs Militaires: C'est Vraiment Très, Très Alarmant!" *La Tribune*, February 20, 2018a. As of April 29, 2020:
https://www.latribune.fr/entreprises-finance/industrie/aeronautique-defense/disponibilite-des-aeronefs-militaires-c-est-vraiment-tres-tres-alarmant-1-3-769078.html

———, "Comment le Ministère des Armées Veut Améliorer la Disponibilité des Avions et des Hélicoptères," *La Tribune*, August 23, 2018b. As of April 30, 2020:
https://www.latribune.fr/entreprises-finance/industrie/aeronautique-defense/comment-le-ministere-des-armees-veut-ameliorer-la-disponibilite-des-avions-et-des-helicopteres-787022.html

Center for Strategic and International Studies, "Global Leaders Forum: H.E. Florence Parly, Minister for the Armed Forces of France," video, YouTube, October 20, 2017. As of September 10, 2020:
https://www.csis.org/events/global-leaders-forum-he-florence-parly-minister-armed-forces-france

Centre National d'Études Spatiales, "CSO/MUSIS," April 9, 2018. As of April 21, 2020:
https://cso.cnes.fr/en/csomusis-0

Chachaty, Helen, "Les Reaper Armés dès Fin 2019 à Niamey," *Le Journal de l'Aviation*, May 22, 2019. As of April 21, 2020:
https://www.journal-aviation.com/actualites/42475-les-reaper-armes-des-fin-2019-a-niamey

Chapleau, Philippe, "MRTT: Florence Parly Accélère la Livraison de 12 Avions Dont le Premier Sera a Istres Mi-Octobre," *Lignes de Défense, Ouest-France*, September 20, 2018. As of April 21, 2020:
http://lignesdedefense.blogs.ouest-france.fr/archive/2018/09/20/mrtt-florence-parly-accelere-la-livraison-de-12-avions-dont-19664.html

———, "Cyberdéfense. L'Armée Passe à l'Offensive," *Ouest-France*, January 18, 2019. As of April 21, 2020:
https://www.ouest-france.fr/politique/defense/cyberdefense-l-armee-francaise-passe-l-offensive-6179782

Chaumont, Jacques, "Avis Présenté au Nom de la Commission des Affaires Etrangères, de la Défense et des Forces Armées, sur le Projet de Loi de Finances Pour 1981, Adopté par l'Assemblée Nationale," Paris: Sénat, November 19, 1980. As of July 2, 2020:
https://www.senat.fr/rap/1980-1981/i1980_1981_0101_06.pdf

Commission de la Défense Nationale et des Forces Armées, Assemblée Nationale, "Audition du Général Jean-Pierre Bosser, Chef D'état-Major de l'Armée de Terre, sur le Projet de Loi de Finances pour 2018," October 11, 2017. As of April 21, 2020:
http://www.assemblee-nationale.fr/15/cr-cdef/17-18/c1718009.asp

Cone, Allen, "Thales to Develop Sonar System for New French Sub," UPI, February 8, 2018. As of April 21, 2020:
https://www.upi.com/Defense-News/2018/02/08/Thales-to-develop-sonar-system-for-new-French-sub/7841518120760

Council on Foreign Relations, "Turla," undated. As of July 22, 2019:
https://www.cfr.org/interactive/cyber-operations/turla

Dancer, Marie, "Nouvelle Commande Française pour le Rafale, Qui Poursuit sa Modernisation," *La Croix*, January 14, 2019.

de Briganti, Giovanni, "Airbus, Dassault Jointly Awarded Two-Year SCAF/FCAS Architecture Study," *Defense-Aerospace*, February 5, 2019.

de Legge, Dominique, "Avis Présenté au Nom de la Commission des Finances Sur le Projet de Loi, Adopté par l'Assemblée Nationale Après Engagement de la Procédure Accélérée, Relative à la Programmation Militaire pour les Années 2019 à 2025 et Portant Diverses Dispositions Intéressant la Défense," *Sénat*, No. 430, May 15, 2018a.

———, "Le Parc d'Hélicoptères des Armées: Une Envolée des Coûts de Maintenance, Une Indisponibilité Chronique, des Efforts Qui Doivent Être Prolongés," *Sénat*, July 11, 2018b.

Defense Industry Daily, "France's Future SSNs: The Barracuda Class," May 10, 2018. As of April 21, 2020:
https://www.defenseindustrydaily.com/frances-future-ssns-the-barracuda-class-02902

Delaporte, Murielle, "From Paris to Orbit: France's New Space Strategy," *Breaking Defense*, January 3, 2019. As of April 21, 2020:
https://breakingdefense.com/2019/01/from-paris-to-orbit-frances-new-space-strategy/

Delerue, François, Alix Desforges, and Aude Géry, "A Close Look at France's New Military Cyber Strategy," *War on the Rocks*, April 23, 2019. As of April 21, 2020: https://warontherocks.com/2019/04/a-close-look-at-frances-new-military-cyber-strategy/

Dorman, Andrew, *The Future of British Defence Policy*, Institut Français de Relations Internationals Security Studies Center, Focus Stratégique No. 74, July 2017. As of May 25, 2020: https://www.ifri.org/sites/default/files/atoms/files/dorman_british_defence_policy_2017.pdf

Élysée, "Déclaration de M. François Hollande, Président de la République, sur la Dissuasion Nucléaire, à Istres le 19 Février 2015," February 19, 2015. As of April 21, 2020: https://www.elysee.fr/francois-hollande/2015/02/19/declaration-de-m-francois-hollande-president-de-la-republique-sur-la-dissuasion-nucleaire-a-istres-le-19-fevrier-2015

———, "Discours du Président Emmanuel Macron sur la Stratégie de Défense et de Dissuasion Devant les Stagiaires de la 27ème Promotion de l'École de Guerre," February 7, 2020.

"Estonia to Contribute to French-Led Operation Barkhane in Mali," *Army Technology*, April 17, 2018. As of April 20, 2020: https://www.army-technology.com/news/estonia-contribute-french-led-operation-barkhane-mali

EU—*See* European Union.

European Union, *Shared Vision, Common Action: A Stronger Europe—A Global Strategy for the European Union's Foreign and Security Policy*, Brussels, June 2016. As of April 21, 2020: https://eeas.europa.eu/sites/eeas/files/eugs_review_web_0.pdf

F. de St V, "L'Artillerie Française—(Quelques Possibles) Tendances pour Demain en Operations 3/3," *Mars Attaque*, July 16, 2018. As of April 21, 2020: http://mars-attaque.blogspot.com/2018/07/lartillerie-francaise-quelques.html

"FANAL 19: 30 Rafale M," *Le Fauteuil de Colbert*, February 12, 2019. As of April 30, 2020: http://lefauteuildecolbert.blogspot.com/2019/02/fanal-19-30-rafale-m.html

Faram, Mark D., "French Aircrews Ready to Train in Norfolk," *Navy Times*, March 27, 2018. As of April 21, 2020: https://www.navytimes.com/news/your-navy/2018/03/27/french-aircrews-ready-to-train-in-norfolk

Fiorenza, Nicholas, "Programmed for the Future: France Country Briefing," *Janes Defence Weekly*, July 18, 2018.

Fort, Olivier, "Lessons Learned from CAESAR Deployment in Iraq," *Fort Sill Fires Bulletin*, September–October 2019, pp. 41–44. As of July 17, 2020: https://sill-www.army.mil/fires-bulletin-archive/archives/2019/sep-oct/sep-oct.pdf

Fourt, Olivier, "Armée Française: Le Porte-Avions Nucléaire, un Outil Présidentiel," *Radio France International*, November 14, 2018.

"France Joins Race to Develop 'Hypersonic' Weapons, After China, Russia and US," Agence France-Presse, January 29, 2019. As of April 20, 2020: https://www.scmp.com/news/world/europe/article/2184025/france-joins-race-develop-hypersonic-weapons-after-china-russia

"French Presidential Candidate Macron Target of Russian 'Fake News,' His Party Chief Claims," *DeutscheWelle*, February 13, 2017. As of April 20, 2020: https://www.dw.com/en/french-presidential-candidate-macron-target-of-russian-fake-news-his-party-chief-claims/a-37531519

Gao, Charlie, "Why France's Own 'Tomahawk' Missile Is in Serious Trouble," *National Interest*, November 19, 2018. As of April 21, 2020: https://nationalinterest.org/blog/buzz/why-frances-own-tomahawk-missile-serious-trouble-36322

Goldfein, Peter, and André Adamson, "The Trilateral Strategic Initiative: A Primer for Developing Future Airpower Cooperation," *Air Force Journal of European, Middle Eastern, and African Affairs*, Spring 2019.

Government of France, "Secrétariat Général de la Mer (SGMER)—Action de l'État en Mer," undated. As of April 21, 2020: https://www.gouvernement.fr/action-de-l-etat-en-mer-sgmer

Granveau, Eliot, "Sondage. Les Français Soutiennent Nos Opérations Extérieures," *Ouest-France*, April 21, 2017.

Groizeleau, Vincent, "FLOTLOG: L'Accord Franco-Italien Signé," *Mer et Marine*, October 25, 2018. As of April 21, 2020: https://www.meretmarine.com/fr/content/flotlog-laccord-franco-italien-signe

Guibert, Nathalie, "La Gestion des Munitions, un Sujet de Tension pour l'Armée Française," *Le Monde*, November 4, 2016. As of April 21, 2020: https://www.lemonde.fr/international/article/2016/11/04/la-france-a-desormais-largue-plus-de-bombes-en-irak-qu-en-libye-en-2011_5025292_3210.html

Hertel, Olivier, "14 Juillet: Le Griffon, Nouveau Blindé High-Tech de l'Armée de Terre," *Sciences et Avenir*, July 14, 2017. As of July 5, 2018: https://www.sciencesetavenir.fr/high-tech/14-juillet-voici-le-griffon-le-nouveau-blinde-high-tech-de-l-armee-de-terre_114699

Howorth, Jolyon, "François Mitterrand and the 'Domaine Réservé': From Cohabitation to the Gulf War," *French Politics and Society*, Vol. 10, No. 1, Winter 1992, pp. 43–58.

Ifop, *Les Indices de Popularité*, January 2013. As of April 21, 2020: https://www.ifop.com/wp-content/uploads/2018/03/2123-1-study_file.pdf

Irish, John, "France Accuses Russia of Spying on Military from Space," Reuters, September 7, 2018. As of April 20, 2020: https://www.reuters.com/article/us-france-russia-security/france-accuses-russia-of-spying-on-military-from-space-idUSKCN1LN1XT

Irish, John, and Sophie Louet, "France Carries Out Rare Simulation of Nuclear Deterrent Strike," Reuters, February 5, 2019. As of April 20, 2020: https://www.reuters.com/article/us-france-nuclear/france-carries-out-rare-simulation-of-nuclear-deterrent-strike-idUSKCN1PU1MK

Jane's Sentinel Security Assessment–Western Europe, "France–Army," October 1, 2018.

Janes, "Defense Budget Overview–France," September 27, 2018a.

———, "France—Army," October 1, 2018b.

———, "France—Navy," March 13, 2019.

———, "France—Navy," March 10, 2020.

Kauranen, Anne, "It's Time for Realism in EU-Russia Ties: France's Macron," Reuters, August 30, 2018. As of April 21, 2020: https://www.reuters.com/article/us-france-finland-defense-russia/its-time-for-realism-in-eu-russia-ties-frances-macron-idUSKCN1LF0UP

Kelly, Fergus, "Mali: Estonia Troops to Begin Operations in Gao," *Defense Post*, August 21, 2018. As of April 21, 2020: https://thedefensepost.com/2018/08/21/estonia-troops-begin-operations-mali

"La Coûteuse Modernisation de la Dissuasion Nucléaire," Agence France-Presse, June 21, 2018. As of April 20, 2020: https://www.lepoint.fr/societe/la-couteuse-modernisation-de-la-dissuasion-nucleaire-21-06-2018-2229213_23.php

Lagneau, Laurent, "Fort Soutien de l'Opinion Publique aux Opérations Menées par les Armées Françaises," *Zone Militaire*, April 21, 2017a.

———, "Irak: En un An, l'Artillerie Française a Tiré Plus de 10.000 Obus Contre les Positions de l'État Islamique," *Zone Militaire*, September 22, 2017b. As of April 21, 2020: http://www.opex360.com/2017/09/22/irak-en-un-lartillerie-francaise-tire-plus-de-10-000-obus-contre-les-positions-de-letat-islamique

———, "La Construction du Prochain Porte-Avions de la Marine Nationale Sera Pleine de Défis," *Zone Militaire*, November 7, 2017c. As of April 21, 2020: http://www.opex360.com/2017/11/07/la-construction-du-prochain-porte-avions-de-la-marine-nationale-sera-pleine-de-defis

———, "Les C-160 Gabriel Seront Remplacés par Trois Avions Falcon de Guerre Électronique," *Zone Militaire*, March 1, 2018a. As of April 21, 2020: http://www.opex360.com/2018/03/01/c-160-gabriel-seront-remplaces-trois-avions-falcon-de-guerre-electronique

———, "La Question de Doter la Marine Nationale d'un ou de Deux Porte-Avions 'Reste Ouverte' Selon Mme Parly," *Zone Militaire*, September 10, 2018b. As of April 21, 2020: http://www.opex360.com/2018/09/10/question-de-doter-marine-nationale-dun-de-deux-porte-avions-reste-ouverte-selon-mme-parly

———, "Le Ministère des Armées Commande 6 Avions de Patrouille Maritime Atlantique 2 Modernisés," *Zone Militaire*, October 24, 2018c. As of April 21, 2020: http://www.opex360.com/2018/10/24/le-ministere-des-armees-commande-6-avions-de-patrouille-maritime-atlantique-2-modernises

———, "La Direction Générale de l'Armement a Prononcé la Qualification du Standard F3-R du Rafale," *Zone Militaire*, November 9, 2018d. As of April 21, 2020: http://www.opex360.com/2018/11/09/la-direction-generale-de-larmement-a-prononce-la-qualification-du-standard-f3-r-du-rafale

———, "Syrie: La Marine Nationale a Tiré les Enseignements des Ratés de l'Opération Hamilton," *Zone Militaire*, November 30, 2018e. As of April 21, 2020: http://www.opex360.com/2018/11/03/syrie-marine-nationale-a-tire-les-enseignements-des-rates-de-loperation-hamilton

Lamigeon, Vincent, "56% des Aéronefs Incapables de Voler : L'Incroyable Talon d'Achille de l'Armée Française," *Challenges*, December 11, 2017.

———, "Budget des Armées 2019: Qui Sont les Gagnants?" *Challenges*, September 27, 2018.

Lasconjarias, Guillaume, and Florent de Saint Victor, "Chasing Grandeur? What You Need to Know About the 2017 French Strategic Review," *War on the Rocks*, October 27, 2017. As of April 21, 2020: https://warontherocks.com/2017/10/chasing-grandeur-what-you-need-to-know-about-the-2017-french-strategic-review/

"Le General de Villiers Revient sur Sa Démission Fracassante dans un Livre," Agence France-Presse, November 7, 2017. As of April 20, 2020: https://www.nouvelobs.com/politique/20171107.AFP2696/le-general-de-villiers-revient-sur-sa-demission-fracassante-dans-un-livre.html

Leicester, John, and Sylvie Corbet, "France Says Russia Satellite Spied in 'Star Wars' Hostility," Associated Press, September 7, 2018. As of April 29, 2020: https://apnews.com/3eb6e868cdec44f08dca288a034dff86/France-says-Russia-satellite-spied-in-%27Star-Wars%27-hostility

Louet, Sophie, "France Commits to Boosting Defense Spending by 35 Percent over Six Years," Reuters, February 8, 2018. As of April 20, 2020: https://www.reuters.com/article/us-france-defence/france-commits-to-boosting-defense-spending-by-35-percent-over-six-years-idUSKBN1FS18Q

Macron, Emmanuel, "Initiative for Europe," speech at the Sorbonne University, Paris, September 26, 2017. As of April 29, 2020: http://international.blogs.ouest-france.fr/archive/2017/09/29/macron-sorbonne-verbatim-europe-18583.html

———, "Déclaration de M. Emmanuel Macron, Président de la République, sur la Defense Européenne à Helsinki le 30 Août 2018," speech in Helsinki, August 30, 2018.

Mallet, Victor, and Mehreen Khan, "Macron Lays Out Proposals for a More 'Protective' EU," *Financial Times*, March 4, 2019.

Mallory, King, Gene Germanovich, Jonathan William Welburn, and Troy D. Smith, *Burdensharing and Its Discontent: Understanding and Optimizing Allied Contributions to the Collective Defense*, Santa Monica, Calif.: RAND Corporation, 2020. Not available to the general public.

Martinat, Philippe, "Syrie: Des Rates Dans l'Opération Hamilton," *Le Parisien*, April 20, 2018.

McAuley, James, "French President Macron Blasts Russian State-Owned Media as 'Propaganda,'" *Washington Post*, May 29, 2017.

Menanteau, Christian, and Loic Farge, "Armée : Florence Parly S'Attaque aux Défaillances de la Maintenance des Avions," *RTL Radio*, December 12, 2017.

Merchet, Jean-Dominique, "Pologne: Les Militaires Français Ont du Mal à Regarder Vers l'Est," *L'Opinion*, June 12, 2016. As of April 29, 2020: https://www.lopinion.fr/edition/international/pologne-militaires-francais-ont-mal-a-regarder-vers-l-est-104138

———, "Chaudières et Catapultes: Les Enjeux Techniques du Prochain Porte-Avions," *Secret Défense*, January 27, 2017. As of April 29, 2020: https://www.lopinion.fr/blog/secret-defense/chaudieres-catapultes-enjeux-techniques-prochain-porte-avions-119230

———, "Florence Parly Révèle une Cyberattaque Très Sérieuse Contre les Armées," *Secret Défense*, January 18, 2019. As of April 29, 2020: https://www.lopinion.fr/blog/secret-defense/florence-parly-revele-cyberattaque-tres-serieuse-contre-armees-175039

Ministère des Armées, *2018 Defense Key Figures*, Paris, undated.

———, "Question No. 4412 de M. François Carnut-Gentille au Ministère des Armées," January 9, 2018a.

———, "La Cyberdéfense," October 17, 2018b. As of April 21, 2020:
https://www.defense.gouv.fr/portail/enjeux2/la-cyberdefense/la-cyberdefense/presentation

———, *Stratégie Spatiale de Défense*, Paris, 2019.

Ministère des Armées, Actualités, "[Focus] La Posture Permanente de Sûreté Aérienne," February 20, 2016. As of April 21, 2020:
https://www.defense.gouv.fr/actualites/operations/focus-la-posture-permanente-de-surete-aerienne

———, *Les Chiffres Clés de la Défense 2018*, Paris, 2018.

———, "Florence Parly Dévoile la Stratégie Spatiale Française de Défense," January 9, 2020. As of April 21, 2020:
https://www.defense.gouv.fr/actualites/articles/florence-parly-devoile-la-strategie-spatiale-francaise-de-defense

Ministère des Armées, Armée de Terre, "Qui Sommes-Nous?" undated. As of April 21, 2020:
https://www.defense.gouv.fr/terre/l-armee-de-terre/qui-sommes-nous

———, "Opération Daguet: L'Armée de Terre dans la Guerre du Golfe," February 11, 2011. As of July 2, 2020:
https://www.defense.gouv.fr/terre/actu-terre/archives/operation-daguet-l-armee-de-terre-dans-la-guerre-du-golfe

———, "Canon 155 AUF1," July 13, 2016. As of April 20, 2020:
https://www.defense.gouv.fr/terre/equipements/vehicules/canon-155-auf1

———, "VBCI—Véhicule Blindé de Combat de l'Infanterie," July 12, 2017. As of April 30, 2020:
https://www.defense.gouv.fr/fre/terre/equipements/vehicules/vbci-vehicule-blinde-de-combat-de-l-infanterie

———, "AMX 10 RC Renové," October 25, 2018. As of April 20, 2020:
https://www.defense.gouv.fr/terre/equipements/vehicules/amx-10-rc-renove

———, "JAGUAR," January 30, 2019a. As of April 21, 2020:
https://www.defense.gouv.fr/terre/equipements/scorpion/scorpion/6-operations/jaguar

———, "GRIFFON," July 15, 2019b. As of April 20, 2020:
https://www.defense.gouv.fr/terre/equipements/vehicules/scorpion/griffon

———, "CAESAR," January 28, 2020. As of April 20, 2020:
https://www.defense.gouv.fr/terre/equipements/vehicules/caesar-camion-equipe-d-un-systeme-d-artillerie

Ministère des Armées, Direction Générale de l'Armement, "Le Système de Lutte Anti-Mines Marines Future (SLAMF)," March 24, 2016. As of April 21, 2020: https://www.defense.gouv.fr/english/dga/equipement/naval/le-systeme-de-lutte-anti-mines-marines-futur-slamf

———, "Création de l'Agence de l'Innovation de Defense et Nomination d'Emmanuel Chiva au Poste de Directeur," September 5, 2018. As of April 30, 2020: https://www.defense.gouv.fr/dga/actualite/creation-de-l-agence-de-l-innovation-de-defense-et-nomination-d-emmanuel-chiva-au-poste-de-directeur

Ministère des Armées, Opérations, "Opération Sentinelle," undated. As of July 1, 2019: https://www.defense.gouv.fr/operations/france/operation-sentinelle

———, "EAP: Fin de Mandat pour l'Armée Française," August 30, 2018. As of April 20, 2020: https://www.defense.gouv.fr/operations/otan/eap/eap-fin-de-mandat-pour-l-armee-francaise

———, "Déploiements Opérationnels des Forces Armées Françaises," January 22, 2019a. As of April 21, 2020: https://www.defense.gouv.fr/operations/rubriques_complementaires/carte-des-operations-et-missions-militaires

———, "CHAMMAL: Task Force Wagram, 8 Mandats s'Illustrent dans la Lutte Contre Daech," May 3, 2019b. As of July 17, 2020: https://www.defense.gouv.fr/operations/actualites2/chammal-task-force-wagram-8-mandats-s-illustrent-dans-la-lutte-contre-daech

———, "Mission Lynx," August 28, 2019c. As of April 21, 2020: https://www.defense.gouv.fr/operations/otan/efp/dossier-de-presentation/mission-lynx

———, "Opération Barkhane," March 30, 2020. As of July 17, 2020: https://www.defense.gouv.fr/operations/barkhane/dossier-de-reference/operation-barkhane

Ministère de l'Europe et des Affaires Étrangères, "Australia, France Join to Build Space Industry Capability," September 18, 2018. As of April 21, 2020: https://au.ambafrance.org/Australia-France-join-to-build-space-industry-capability

Mongin, Dominique, "Genèse de l'Armement Nucléaire Français," *Revue Historique des Armées*, No. 262, 2011, pp. 14–26.

NATO—*See* North Atlantic Treaty Organization.

Noël, Jean-Christophe, Morgan Paglia, and Elie Tenenbaum, *Les Armées Françaises Face aux Menaces Anti-Aériennes de Nouvelle Génération*, Paris: French Institute of International Relations, No. 86, December 2018.

North Atlantic Treaty Organization, "Financial and Economic Data Relating to NATO Defense," press release, PR/CP(2011)027, March 10, 2011.

———, "Defence Expenditures of NATO Countries (2011–2018)," press release, PR-CP(2019)034, March 14, 2019a.

———, "Alliance Ground Surveillance," updated June 21, 2019b. As of April 29, 2020:
https://www.nato.int/cps/en/natolive/topics_48892.htm

Nossiter, Adam, David E. Sanger, and Nicole Perlroth, "Hackers Came, but the French Were Prepared," *New York Times*, May 9, 2017. As of May 2, 2020:
https://www.nytimes.com/2017/05/09/world/europe/hackers-came-but-the-french-were-prepared.html

Notin, Jean-Christophe, *La Guerre de la France au Mali*, Paris: Tallandier, 2014.

OpinionWay for Cevipof/SciencesPo, "En Qu(o)i les Français Ont-Ils Confiance Aujourd'hui?" January 2019.

Parly, Florence, "Statement on Space Defense," speech in Toulouse, France, September 7, 2018.

———, "The US-French Relationship in a Changing World," speech before the Atlantic Council, Washington, D.C., March 18, 2019a, As of September 12, 2020:
https://www.defense.gouv.fr/fre/actualites/international/discours-a-l-atlantic-council-the-us-french-relationship-in-a-changing-world

———, speech at the 53rd Paris Air Show, June 20, 2019b.

Pennetier, Marine, "Macron Souhaite 'Réenclencher Une Dynamique' avec Poutine Avant le G7," Reuters, June 11, 2019. As of April 20, 2020:
https://fr.reuters.com/article/idFRKCN1TC2CY-OFRTP

Pew Research Center, "Image of Putin, Russia Suffers Internationally," December 6, 2018. As of September 29, 2020:
https://www.pewresearch.org/global/2018/12/06/image-of-putin-russia-suffers-internationally/

"Race for Hypersonic Weapons Heats Up as France Joins 'Stealth by Speed' Contest," Agence France-Presse, January 29, 2019. As of April 20, 2020:
https://www.kaskus.co.id/thread/5c505ed7a2d195611202b2f1/race-for-hypersonic-weapons-heats-up-as-france-joins-stealth-by-speed-contest

République Française, *Defense and National Security Strategic Review*, 2017a.

———, *Strategic Review of Defence and National Security 2017—Key Points*, 2017b.

Roche, Nicolas, *Pourquoi la Dissuasion*, Paris: Presses Universitaires de France, 2017.

Rosnoblet, Jean-François, "Le *Charles de Gaulle*, un Porte-Avions Taillé pour la Guerre et la Diplomatie," Reuters, March 8, 2019.

Scott, Richard, "Euronaval 2018: Integration Activity Ramps Up for French/UK MMCM Programme," *Janes Navy International*, October 23, 2018.

Secrétariat Général de la Défense et la Sécurité Nationale, *Revue Stratégique de Cyberdéfense*, Paris, February 12, 2018.

Seligman, Lara, "Britain, France, Agree to Send Additional Troops to Syria," *Foreign Policy*, July 9, 2019.

Semo, Marc, "Macron Assume Son Virage Russe," *Le Monde*, September 7, 2019.

Sénat, "Equipement de l'Armée Française en Chars de Combat—Sénat," 1990. As of July 2, 2020:
https://www.senat.fr/questions/base/1990/qSEQ900811332.html

———, *2% du PIB: Les Moyens de la Défense Nationale*, May 2017a.

———, *Rapport d'information Fait au Nom de la Commission des Affaires Etrangères, de la Défense et des Forces Armées (1) Par le Groupe de Travail "Les Drones dans les Forces Armées,"* Paris, May 23, 2017b.

———, *Rapport d'Information Fait au Nom de la Commission des Finances (1) Sur la Disponibilité des Hélicoptères du Ministère des Armées*, Paris, July 11, 2018a.

———, Hearing of Navy Chief of Staff Admiral Christophe Prazuck on the 2019 Budget Draft Law, October 9, 2018b.

———, Hearing of Chief of the Joint Staff General François Lecointre on the 2019 Draft Budget Law, October 10, 2018c.

———, Hearing of Defense Minister Florence Parly on the 2019 Draft Budget Law, October 15, 2018d.

———, Hearing of French Air Force Chief of Staff General Philippe Lavigne on the 2019 Draft Budget Law, October 24, 2018e.

Shevin-Coetzee, Michelle, *The European Deterrence Initiative*, Washington, D.C.: Center for Strategic and Budgetary Assessments, 2019.

Shirbon, Estelle, "France's Sarkozy Secures Constitutional Reform," Reuters, July 21, 2008. As of April 30, 2020:
https://www.reuters.com/article/us-france-reform/frances-sarkozy-secures-constitutional-reform-idUSL2182185220080721

Shlapak, David A., and Michael W. Johnson, *Reinforcing Deterrence on NATO's Eastern Flank*, Santa Monica, Calif.: RAND Corporation, RR-1253-A, 2016. As of May 2, 2020:
https://www.rand.org/t/RR1253.html

Shurkin, Michael, *The Abilities of the British, French, and German Armies to Generate and Sustain Armored Brigades in the Baltics*, Santa Monica, Calif.: RAND Corporation, RR-1629-A, 2017. As of April 30, 2020:
https://www.rand.org/t/RR1629.html

"Sondage: 75% des Français Soutiennent l'Intervention au Mali," *Le Parisien*, January 15, 2013. As of April 20, 2020:
http://www.leparisien.fr/international/sondage-75-de-francais-soutiennent-l-intervention-au-mali-15-01-2013-2483685.php

Sprenger, Sebastian, "Germany Unveils Growth Plan for the Bundeswehr," *Defense News*, September 5, 2018. As of May 26, 2020:
https://www.defensenews.com/global/europe/2018/09/05/germany-unveils-growth-plan-for-the-bundeswehr

———, "French Air Force Rehearses a Long-Range Nuclear Strike," *Defense News*, February 5, 2019a. As of April 30, 2020:
https://www.defensenews.com/global/europe/2019/02/05/french-air-force-rehearses-a-long-range-nuclear-strike

———, "More Money, More Missions: German Defense Minister Unveils Her Plan for the Bundeswehr," *Defense News*, November 7, 2019b. As of May 26, 2020:
https://www.defensenews.com/global/europe/2019/11/07/more-money-more-missions-german-defense-minister-unveils-her-plan-for-the-bundeswehr/

Stockholm International Peace Research Institute, *Trends in International Arms Transfers, 2018*, fact sheet, March 2019.

Stokes, Bruce, "NATO's Image Improves on Both Sides of the Atlantic: European Faith in American Military Support Largely Unchanged," Pew Research Center, May 23, 2017. As of April 30, 2020:
https://www.pewresearch.org/global/2017/05/23/natos-image-improves-on-both-sides-of-atlantic

Thierry, Gabriel, "Ces Opérations Venues du Froid Qui Inquiètent Florence Parly," *L'Essor*, January 21, 2019.

Toucas, Boris, "Understanding the Implications of France's Strategic Review on Defense and National Security," Center for Strategic and International Studies, October 19, 2017. As of April 30, 2020:
https://www.csis.org/analysis/understanding-implications-frances-strategic-review-defense-and-national-security

Tran, Pierre, "France Receives Missiles, Launchers to Replace Milan Anti-Tank System," *Defense News*, November 30, 2017a. As of April 30, 2020:
https://www.defensenews.com/land/2017/11/30/france-receives-missiles-launchers-to-replace-milan-anti-tank-system

———, "France Creates Office to Improve Military Aircraft Readiness," *Defense News*, December 12, 2017b. As of April 30, 2020:
https://www.defensenews.com/air/2017/12/12/france-creates-office-to-improve-military-aircraft-readiness

———, "France Takes Delivery of Its 5th FREMM," *Defense News*, July 25, 2018a. As of April 30, 2020:
https://www.defensenews.com/naval/2018/07/25/france-takes-delivery-of-its-5th-fremm

———, "France Wants to Buy Airbus Tankers Sooner," *Defense News*, September 21, 2018b. As of April 30, 2020:
https://www.defensenews.com/global/europe/2018/09/21/france-wants-to-buy-airbus-tankers-sooner

Vavasseur, Xavier, "French Carrier Strike Group Begins 'Foch' Deployment," *USNI News*, January 23, 2020. As of April 30, 2020:
https://news.usni.org/2020/01/23/french-carrier-strike-group-begins-foch-deployment

Viscusi, Gregory, "French Ministers Visit Moscow in First Such Meeting Since 2014," *Bloomberg*, September 8, 2019. As of April 30, 2020:
https://www.bloomberg.com/news/articles/2019-09-08/french-ministers-visit-moscow-in-first-such-meeting-since-2014

Voilquin, Albert, "Rapport d'Information fait au Nom de la Commission des Affaires Étrangères, de la Défense et des Forces Armées (1) en Application de l'Article 22, premier alinéa, du Règlement, sur la force aérienne tactique (F.A.T.A.C)," Sénat, October 10, 1990.

White, Andrew, "Thales Readies Antares for French Army," *Janes International Defence Review*, February 14, 2018.

White House, "Remarks by President Trump and President Macron of France in Joint Press Conference," April 24, 2018. As of April 30, 2020:
https://www.whitehouse.gov/briefings-statements/remarks-president-trump-president-macron-france-joint-press-conference

Witney, Nick, "Macron and the European Intervention Initiative: Erasmus for Soldiers?" European Council on Foreign Relations, May 22, 2018. As of April 30, 2020:
https://www.ecfr.eu/article/commentary_macron_and_the_european_intervention_initiative_erasmus_for_sold